What Others Are Saying

Finally, a parenting book that owns the fact that we as parents cannot control who our children become. Refreshingly candid and deeply reassuring, with a unique perspective on what it means to do daily family life in the presence of Immanuel, the living God-With-Us.

Karen Struble, Ph.D., Clinical Child Psychologist, Private Practice, Hillsborough, NC

Few things are as difficult in life as raising children — especially if you want them to have joy! In the *4 Keys to Parent Fearlessly* book, Toni beautifully shares her life, struggles, fears and joys to inspire us. Toni's stories are the best! Now and then you read a book that changes the way you think. Well, this is the book every parent needs. I could not put down Toni's book once I picked it up. Buy several copies and give them away!

Chris Coursey, President of THRIVEtoday and Author of *The Joy Switch*

Refreshingly honest and beautifully transparent! Toni masterfully captures the heart of parenting, and forges a path in which parents are empowered and equipped to raise children from a heart-to-heart connection. Backed by scripture and grounded in Jesus, *4 Keys to Parent Fearlessly* is truly a book for everyone who finds themselves investing in the life of a child.

Taylor Garaguso, Mother of two

This book condenses the best brain science, scriptural wisdom, and relational practices in a brief, yet potent read. I am strengthened and encouraged by Toni's storytelling as well as her integration of such depth and knowledge. Parents of any age would greatly benefit from reading this book. As you read this book, I see blessings of healing and wholeness happening for you as you desire to learn to parent with love and wisdom.

John Loppnow, Relationship Coach / Therapist
www.LoppnowRelationshipCenter.com

"DON'T BUY THIS BOOK! ...If you are looking for a few easy steps that guarantee that all of your children will turn out as perfect, Christian adults. On the other hand, if you are far enough into parenting to know that the actual journey often is messy, disorienting and even frightening, this book is for you. In it, Toni tells the story of her journey with Jesus through the disasters and delights of parenting. You will learn from her how to be both "joy fueled" and "Jesus led" in the midst of real life. I've walked with Toni and her husband, Matt, in community for the last seven years; I know that this is not just theory for her. It's how she lives.

John White, Co-founder/Director, LK10, co-author of *Joy Fueled: Catalyzing a Revolution of Joyful Communities*

Whatever I read by Toni Daniels breathes life into my soul. This book is no exception. Her deep vulnerability and remarkable tenacity with parenting inspire me to follow suit. Beyond that, she offers simple but powerful tools for connecting with the heart of my middle and high schoolers that were definitely not in my toolbox. Read this if you want renewed and retooled!

Andy Rittenhouse, Co-founder, Vital Families

Are you looking for a book to help your children score better on the ACT? Be popular and successful? Or make sure they don't experiment with drugs or alcohol or sex? If so, this is NOT the book for you. If you are like me, and you realize that your children are human, that they will make both good and bad decisions, that there will be relational conflicts in your home, and that you are not a perfect parent, then this book has some gems for you. As a parent of four adult sons, and grandparent of seven, I can attest to the fact that, as parents and grandparents, we are not in control of what happens to our children or how they respond to the difficulties of life. We can, however, learn valuable truths from Toni Daniels as she shares what she has learned, the things she puts into practice daily, as she and her husband raise three children. Do they have problems? Yes. Do they have relational issues? Yes. If you choose to read this book you will learn how, together with God, Toni and her family work through these things and return to joy. With the examples she shares, you will learn skills that can be applied to your own family.

John Shaw, "Dad" and "Gamp"

Fear is the great immobilizer of every parent. It clamps its vice around us and refuses to leave. Toni's wisdom will enable you face the lies you believe as a parent and release the shackles of fear that have kept you in bondage. Reading her words will help you extend grace to your own heart and actions.

Brian Housman, Executive Director, 360Family, parenting coach, and author of *How You Always Meant to Parent*

The palette of God's revelation is infinite—and customized for each beloved child of God. If you want to increase your capacity to join God in parenting your own family, this book is for you. Toni brings to light the hard-won wisdom and experience of a skilled parent practitioner in the Joy-Fueled, Jesus-Led way.

Dr. Kent Smith, Co-founder, LK10, co-author of *Joy Fueled: Catalyzing a Revolution of Joyful Communities*

Toni issues the challenge to *Parent Fearlessly*, but she doesn't leave us alone with the challenge. She provides warm, loving guidance and examples of how to recognize our fear, really connect with our Comforter, move from fear to joy, and look for solutions from this incredible place of joy. It is possible - I've seen it in Toni's home, and I've applied it in my own life. This little book is worth its weight in gold because it was mined from experience and a determined perseverance towards joy.

Amy Brown, Author of *Relational Skills in the Bible* and *Journey Groups: A relational discipleship experience*

4 Keys to
Parent
Fearlessly

*Staying
Joy Fueled and Jesus Led,
Even When You Can't
Control the Outcome*

Toni M. Daniels

Copyright

4 Keys to Parent Fearlessly

Staying Joy Fueled and Jesus Led, Even When You Can't Control the Outcome

Copyright © 2021 Toni M Daniels

All rights reserved. No part of this publication may be reproduced, distributed, or transmitted in any form or by any means, including photocopying, recording, or other electronic or mechanical methods, without the prior written permission of the publisher, except in the case of brief quotations embodied in reviews and certain other non-commercial uses permitted by copyright law.

Unless otherwise specified, all scripture is from the NIV version, all rights reserved.

ISBN: 978-1-7346840-3-2

Cover Design: Darko Bovan, 99desings.com

Edited/Layout by: Jim Bryson

(JamesLBryson@gmail.com)

Proofreading by: Tammy Lancaster

Dedication

To Allie Elin Daniels, aka Luna.

For all the years I was fear driven instead of Love led, I'm sorry. Raising you trained me, matured me and made me the woman I am today.

I love you and delight in you with all of my heart.

Contents

All Is Found xv
Introduction 1
Part 1 Dismantling Our Parenting Fears 9
1. A Mysterious Collaborative Parenting Relationship ... 11
2. Recognizing Fear 23
3. Realizing You Are Not Alone 43
4. Receiving Truth 57
5. Responding By Co-creating New Realities 69
6. Fear Dismantling In Action 77
Part 2 Building a Resilient Family 91
7. Parenting As Children of God 93
8. Recognizing Feelings Are Active 97
9. Reassuring Your Children They Are Not Alone 105
10. Recapturing and Redirecting Attention to Truth 109
11. Reaffirming Their Resilience 121
12. Resilience Building in Action 133
Resources 145
About the Author 149

Acknowledgements

THIS BOOK BEGAN AS A BRAIN-STORMING SESSION with my amazingly talented niece, Taylor Garaguso. Taylor, I am indebted to you for helping get this off the ground and look forward to one day writing with you!

Thank you, Ulher family, for a writer's getaway on the Santa Barbara beach complete with deep relational connection and the most exhilarating night I have ever had dancing and singing at a piano bar.

Sandy Fitzpatrick, Hilary Kline, and Matthew Daniels: you three hold me more than you know. Sandy, your encouragement that day on the San Diego beach made me believe that maybe this really was worth sharing with others.

Celebrating every day's writing victory was my cheerleading team: Matthew, my husband, and our two youngest, Anne and Matt. You all make me dance and smile!

If it were not for Jim Bryson, my friend and editor, this may have been on a shelf for years before seeing the light of day. Thank you for your strong words of affirmation that lit a fire under my feet.

And finally, I want to recognize my launch team members who worked tirelessly for weeks to make sure this book gets into the hands of parents everywhere. Longing to see parents more joy fueled and Jesus led, this team supported me, cheered me on, and shared the joy of introducing *4 Keys to Parent Fearlessly* to the world.

Thank you, Ryan Paterson, Hilary Kline, John White, Sandy Fitzpatrick, Marty Uhler, Mark Richardson, Matthew Daniels, Jason Twombly, Susan Ramsey, Billie Brackeen, Matthew Daniels, Karen Smith, Yvonne Powell, Amy Reinhardt and Dr. Karen Struble.

All Is Found

Rain.

The storm beats down.
Thunder shakes our bones.
Lightning flashes all our fears.
Trees snap and threaten to sweep us away.
Who will survive this storm?

We hold on to each other for dear life
And huddle the kids between us.
Yet one of them is still out there.
I see fear grip my husband's eyes
As he too is torn from us.
Tears cover my face.

No one wants this.
No one wants to be this helpless.

I fight to quiet my thoughts.
Strength wells from the core of my being
It moves through my body.
My spine straightens
Peace radiates a shield around us.

Even here, in the storm, we are secure.
It will not destroy us,
Only shake all that was meant to be shaken.
It shakes for days.

Then peace, quiet.

I survey the damage.
The lost one has been found.
She comes running.

My husband fought for days
And finds his way back to us.
The house we built is gone,
But it was not safe anyway.

We set to rebuild, stronger,
A dwelling that can withstand
The storms we know are coming.
And we work together
More resilient than before.

For we have not lost each other.
We have found ourselves.

Toni M Daniels
February 2020

Introduction

The Fears We Carry

WHEN I BECAME A MOTHER AT 27, one would have thought that I was ready to take on the task. By then I had earned a master's degree in Leadership Development, had been in ministry for nine years, and had completed a one-year overseas mission experience. I had faced brokenness in myself and those around me, had found healing for much of my past trauma, and helped countless number of people begin healthy relationships with God and with each other. One would have thought my Allie would be raised to perfection!

And yet, as I held this newborn in my arms, fear gripped me. I didn't want her to ever experience pain. God had entrusted this tiny life to me; she was my responsibility. The weight of failing crushed me.

What did I know about parenting? I was the baby of the family and had never seen adults raise younger children. I had never even worked with children, nor had I ever wanted to. I loved a world that I could control, where I could drive the outcomes, where I was in charge, where people came to me because they wanted my help and would generally do what I said.

This parenting thing, however, was a totally different situation. As Allie cried and cried, and I frantically searched for reasons why, I knew I was not in control. I could not control her body or her feelings. How could I make her eat or sleep when I wanted her to? What would make her reflux go away or keep her from vomiting? And how was I supposed to stop her tears? The child I hoped would never experience pain was suffering in my arms and I was powerless to stop it.

I could not control my own emotions either. My response to helplessness surprised me. Anger could swell up within me without warning, resulting in a flood of tears having their way with me.

In desperation, I grabbed every parenting book I could find. I just knew that if I learned to parent properly, make correct decisions and do all the right things, my children would turn out healthy, happy and whole.

One book actually promised this. Theirs was the "biblical" way to parent. If I did it their way, they assured me, Allie would turn out a happy, well-established, God-fearing citizen. Finally, here was hope that I could control the outcome! This was the answer I'd been searching for. As nascent parents, my husband, Matt, and I dutifully implemented the book's suggestions, redoubling our efforts when things didn't always go as planned. It took two years of our precious baby's life to realize this method wasn't working. In fact, it was a disaster.

As I look back 20 years later, I wonder if it was those two years of applying the book's "biblical model" that actually wounded Allie the most. Maybe it was our ineptitude in implementing it; maybe it was the fallacy of the method. In all likelihood, it was the combination of the two and other factors we are only just discovering today.

Introduction

While we will never fully know the exact damage this parenting model inflicted, the reality is that the method did not help us mature as parents, nor did it equip us for what was ahead. It was all about doing the right things, maintaining control and working a system. It never mentioned important things like attuning to your child's needs, trusting your intuition or quieting yourself to sense God's presence to comfort and guide you. I would not discover these relational ideas until many years later. No, this parenting philosophy was all about following rules so that your child would turn our right...whatever that meant.

I so wish someone would have told me that parenting is not about controlling the outcomes but being present in the moment. That it is not about ensuring that our children always make the right choices but supporting them without fear when they don't. That while there is no fool-proof method, and none of our children will escape the effects of brokenness in this world, we don't have to fear that brokenness. There is a way to parent with peace and joy fueling us instead of fear.

Maybe someone did tell me and I was not ready to hear it because I still wanted to believe I could control the outcomes.

Because the relational path is so foreign to us, we accept the guarantees to stay in control. Often, we can't comprehend relationship as a viable means of child raising, even when someone tries to show us the way. We fear messing up our children with our inept parenting, and we fear bad things happening to them, so we clamp down tightly to eliminate all variables.

At the writing of this introduction, the *#me too* campaign swept the United States. Thousands of abusers were exposed for sexually exploiting adults and children alike. It is especially disturbing to realize that abusers have preyed on our children even with parents unaware in the same room.

We have been gripped as never before with the fear that at any moment, in any situation, our child could be the next victim of sexual harm inflicted by an adult or another child. This fear is not without merit. My own small children suffered attempted harmful encounters at school, at birthday parties, while playing with neighborhood children, and even at church. Many parents I know share similar experiences.

I have also joined the ranks of parents—hundreds of thousands of good, loving people—who have watched their teenage child turn to drugs, self-harm, and/or illicit sexual encounters to numb their pain in a world gone wrong.

Horrified, we struggle to protect our children and keep them as safe as possible, all the while fearing what could still happen right under our noses. Our children could be abused or worse—abuse someone else. They could rebel, turn away from our values, embrace drugs or toxic relationships, drawing from addictions what we could not give them, what they apparently need. We fear losing not just control, but our children themselves.

Maybe you're afraid your child won't be popular, won't make the grade, won't win the game, won't apply themselves, will marry the wrong person, will be attracted

Introduction

to the "wrong" sex, or identify with a different gender identity.

Maybe your fears are not that dramatic, but they are there nonetheless—a car accident or a broken arm from climbing a tree, a concussion, or even ADD.

Regardless of the depth of your fear, it is there. I know it. I feel it too.

That small, beautiful baby nestled in my arms went on to experience everything I feared most: sexual trauma, bullying, self-harm, attempted suicide, mental illness, drug addiction and teenage pregnancy. No amount of fear-fueled, control parenting could have prevented it. In fact, as long as I feared what could happen, I was unable to find stable ground from which to lead my family.

Ten years into our parenting endeavor with Allie, Matt and I welcomed Anne and Matthew into our family. Then, just a few years after that, we adopted a 23-year-old, Hilary.

Thankfully, as our family has grown, we have learned a better, freer way to parent, one that puts relationship first, dismantles fear, and equips us to show up powerfully for our children, no matter what they choose to do, and no matter what happens to them.

Parenting out of joy and peace instead of fear and control has given my children the real protection they need: belonging and resilience, the relational capacity to overcome whatever adversity comes their way. My family has learned experientially that we can withstand anything that comes against us, and that we stand together no matter what.

In this life of parenting, there are no guarantees that our children will be safe or that they will choose a healthy path to deal with the struggles they encounter in their lives. This cannot be our goal because it lies outside of our control. So, if we cannot control the outcomes, what can we control? We can control how we respond to these struggles and how we show up for ourselves and our children. Parenting joy fueled and Jesus led prepares us to meet the challenges head-on with peace and hope, knowing that nothing is beyond God's repair.

While trying to control how your children turn out is a typical parenting approach, this book presents a whole different option for you. This approach involves four keys that will unlock new realities you never knew existed. Adapting my 30 years of working in helping professions, offering relational coaching, prayer-based trauma recovery and leadership training, I take you into my family setting where you will learn to:

1. Recognize when fear is active.
2. Realize you are not alone.
3. Receive Truth's perspective.
4. Respond by co-creating new realities that unlock your family's resilience.

I will show you what this process looks like in some of the most difficult parenting moments any parent could have. And, how it all happens nested in a mysterious collaborative effort with the God who loves us.

Introduction

Trying to control the outcomes of parenting only leaves you gripped by fear at every turn. Are you ready to step into a mysterious, collaborative, relational way of parenting that feels unknown and sometimes out of control but frees you from fear and equips you and your children to bounce back from anything life can throw at you? Are you ready to let go of the need to control every outcome, and parent fearlessly?

It all begins by knowing a redemptive power so encompassing that nothing could ever happen to you or your child that is beyond its repair.

Let's explore this mysterious collaborative parenting relationship.

Part 1

Dismantling Our Parenting Fears

1
A Mysterious Collaborative Parenting Relationship

MY YOUNGEST DAUGHTER, ANNE, WAS THREE YEARS OLD when she started a three-hour-a-day pre-school in Uruguay, South America. Matt and I were social entrepreneurs and church planters based in Uruguay for 15 years. Although Anne was born there, Spanish was still a struggle for her. Those few hours a day would give her the much-needed Spanish boost that she could not get at home.

Our "slow-warmer," as we called her, Anne always had a tough time with new environments, especially crowds. Her temperament was extremely sensitive to external stimuli, and we had to give her extra support in that area. On top of that, when Anne was one, her brother Matt was born ten weeks early. Consequently, I was physically absent for almost two months while caring for him. Even though my husband, Matt, could give full-time care for Anne, my absence took a toll on her ability to regulate or control her emotions that continued to show up for years.

As expected, the first week of school was difficult for Anne, but at least she went without crying. The second week, however, was heart-wrenching. When I dropped her off, my precious baby girl fought to stay with me. The teachers assured me this was a "normal" transition. However, the next morning when I left her screaming at the door of her classroom, my heart broke and questions flooded my mind.

Is this just a normal adjustment period that will pass in time?

Should I pull her out and keep her home for another year?

Are they able to comfort her enough?

Am I a terrible mom?

Overwhelmed, I trudged to my car. Tears flooded my view as I pulled away. I didn't get far. Feeling helpless and alone, I pulled the car over to the side of the road. I struggled to keep from hyperventilating as I heaved with sorrow. After a couple of deep breaths, I scanned my body and found the pit that had formed in my stomach. Adrenaline was wracking my nervous system. My chest was tight, every breath a hard-fought battle. A few more draughts of air and my emotional pain surfaced. Thinking of my little girl in distress crushed me. Like her, I felt helpless and alone, full of fear. *What was I going to do?*

"Papa, Papa," was all I could say. I needed God's presence. I needed His guidance. I quickly went to a beach in my imagination—a place where I often sense the presence of God. I saw an image I knew to be Jesus there with me on the sand. I collapsed at His feet in a quaking heap of tears.

"You love your daughter so much, don't you?" He said as he knelt down to look into my eyes. I shook my head *yes*. He saw into me. He affirmed my heart for my daughter. I felt known, loved, safe.

"What are you afraid of, my child?" His words were not audible, but thoughts like my own, except different, more powerful, living.

My answer tumbled out of me.

"Afraid I have ruined Anne. Afraid she will feel abandoned. Afraid I have been a terrible steward of what you have entrusted to me. She has suffered so much loss already in her three short years, and I carry the weight of that loss. I am so scared of getting it wrong and that it will have permanent negative consequences on her life."

He drew me closer, face to face, kneeling in front of me, cupping my cheeks in his hands. I looked up; his face filled with compassion. He felt my anguish. He was not afraid of my feelings or situation. He was glad to be with me. I was not alone. I wanted to relinquish all my fear.

"What do I need to know?" I pleaded as he lovingly held my gaze.

"Toni, my child, am I bigger than this?" His unexpected question filled my mind like a bright light, extinguishing the darkness.

What did He mean?

The question confronted something within me, hidden and unknown. I knew he understood my heart better than I did. My confused look begged him to continue.

He graciously conceded, "You apparently think that your mistakes have the power to harm Anne so badly that I could not heal her or restore her."

His gentle insight was laser-focused and accurate. I had no idea I was believing this to be true. "You're right," I confessed out loud.

His next question came very clearly to me: "Do you believe I am bigger than this?"

His eyes looked compassionately into the depths of my soul, penetrating and revealing all. Did I believe he could restore, redeem, and repair my little girl, no matter what? He was inviting me to trust Him. I have seen that look many times, that invitation, in my years of knowing Him. And I have never regretted trusting Him. This gave me courage.

"Yes, yes, yes," I sobbed. "Of course, You are bigger than any mistake I can make. Of course, You are bigger than any brokenness that seeks to harm Anne. Yes, yes, yes."

With every *yes*, I felt despair leave, loneliness dissipate and fear subside. With every *yes*, I received Truth, letting in a little more of Him each time.

The truth was, I was not alone. He was with me, and He was bigger than my fear. He was also with Anne. He could heal any wound she suffered. Trust filled my soul and fear had no space left to cling to. Alone in my car, I rested with Jesus, collapsing into His arms. Safely held by

Truth, my heart rate slowed and my mind quieted. Even as he confronted me, His kindness and compassion led me to repentance and trust just as Romans 2:4 says:

> *Or do you despise the riches of His goodness, forbearance, and longsuffering, not knowing that the goodness of God leads you to repentance?*

I was so glad to be held and comforted, confronted and yet calmed. Knowing these truths intellectually is so different from experiencing them relationally. The questions about what to do with Anne still remained, but the intense confusion and fear dissolved. I was at peace, physically and emotionally.

"Papa, am I doing the right thing for her?" I asked. "Will this be more harmful than beneficial? Should we pull her out of school and wait another year to start her when Matt starts? She has suffered so much already. Are they giving her the emotional support she needs?"

The questions came not from desperation but a neutral place of care-giving and responsibility. I wanted to do this with him, not by myself.

In the quiet, I sensed Jesus reply with very direct advice. "Spend time alone with just her each day. While Matt naps, give your full attention to her. Play with her, whatever she wants to play. Watch her and just be with her."

That was it? That was his great plan?

What He was asking of me would be hard. I was always so exhausted by the time she got home that I normally napped when Matt napped. I was not sure how I would do it, but if God said I needed to do it, I would find a way. He would give me strength.

"Okay, Papa, I can do that."

"And don't worry about her at school," He continued. "I, Myself, will comfort her there. Wait and see what happens over the next few days. If you don't see things getting better, we can talk about it again."

His words conveyed an image of Him in the classroom with Anne, accompanying the teacher and bringing peace.

God had attuned to my heart, soothed my fears, and now given me a simple parenting plan that was exactly what Anne needed. I could now respond to this situation as a loving, caring, peaceful, responsible parent. I put the car into drive, feeling confident and supported. The tears were gone, replaced with deep joy, gratitude and quiet determination. I had a plan of action that would carry me through this ordeal…at least for the next few days.

Over the next three days, I spent time after school playing with Anne. She wanted to play with her wooden doll house and her tiny wooden family pieces. As I watched her engage in play, I noticed that she used these figures to act out the issues she was having at school, including the language barrier and the difficulty of making friends. My little introvert rarely interacted with me during these play times, but frequently glanced over her shoulders to make sure I was watching. I really did nothing but pay attention and be present with her. Sometimes I even fell asleep next to her while she was playing, but she didn't seem to mind.

A Mysterious Collaborative Parenting Relationship

At the end of this short experiment, I was relieved to notice Anne was going to school happy and content. It worked!

About a week later, as I was dropping her off, the teacher pulled me aside and asked in amazement, "What happened to Anne? What did you do?"

I was puzzled, not sure what she was referring to.

"Anne has turned 180 degrees since last week and is happily integrating here at school. There is no fear, no hesitation. She is doing incredibly well."

Joy welled up inside of me. While I was not sure how the teacher would respond, I decided to share with her what had happened just a week before, how I had sensed God with me, guiding me, and giving me a plan to play alone with Anne each day. I told her that He had assured me that He himself was going to be with Anne at school, taking care of her, comforting her.

"So," I finished explaining. "I guess she feels Jesus here in your classroom with her, and she is happy!"

"I have goosebumps," the teacher replied as she rubbed her arms. Then she smiled, surveyed her classroom and turned back to me with tears in her eyes, "To think Jesus Himself is in my classroom! I am honored! I knew some miracle was happening!"

Her tears were contagious. We hugged, and I walked away feeling deeply satisfied that God's plan was so much better than anything I could have come up with on my own, especially in my fear.

*****

When we get overwhelmed as parents, what happens within us is crucial. Unfortunately, most of us never slow down enough to realize what is happening. We usually go on autopilot and handle our emotions by letting them drive our actions. On any given day, my autopilot of fear might have led me to:

- Talk myself into a better place by rationalizing that this is normal for a child adjusting and that Anne is probably settling in by now and will be okay.
- Rush back, make a rash decision to pull her out of school until she is older.
- Shut my emotions down altogether, disconnect from the pain and lose myself in work for the day, effectively ignoring the problem.
- Carry the helplessness and fear into my day and make myself physically sick with worry.
- Call someone to help me calm down and see things logically, knowing there is no guarantee they will understand, comfort me or guide me correctly. Most likely, I would overwhelm them with my own emotions.

What we often miss is that there is another option to parenting that leads to peace and creativity, but it requires us to slow down and process what we are feeling, so fear does not take charge. Many times, however, reacting out of our emotions is the more obvious and natural-feeling option when parenting becomes overwhelming. We may try to dismiss the fear, disconnect from it if we can, but if that does not work, we make rash decisions, overwhelm others, or obsess into worry, doubt, guilt, shame and physical illness.

None of these ways of reacting bring true peace, nor do they help us solve the problem at hand. On the contrary, they often complicate our lives even further by causing physical stress, disconnection and overwhelming the relationships around us.

The good news is that there is another option. That is what this book is about. Looking back over countless failures that eventually gave way to an increasing track record of successes, what I was led to practice can be summed up in four steps (or keys). I suppose it is because our brains are pattern-making machines that my brain somehow managed to classify these steps with four "R words." (If that sort of thing is not your cup of tea, I beg you to indulge me.) These four Rs have become a game-changing framework that never fails to lead me to connection, wholeness, peace and creativity. It is the road less taken, the path easily missed. Unless someone points it out to us, we might not know it's there. The 4 keys to unlocking this path are:

- Recognize
- Realize
- Receive
- Respond

Better explained, we:

- Recognize when fear is active
- Realize we are not alone
- Receive truth that dissipates fear
- Respond by co-creating new realities

As illustrated by my story of Anne, we cannot forge this path alone. Rather, it is the result of a mysterious cooperation with the Creator of the Universe who makes co-creating new realities possible. Tapping into *the s*ource of joy and peace individually and communally not only helps us dismantle our fear, but gives us creative ideas for how to view struggles, solve problems and build resilient families. Applying these keys or forging these steps with the Divine results in an empowered response to unimaginable situations, as you will see in the following chapters.

Now, these keys, do not necessarily happen linearly. Consider them as four necessary *components* to dismantle the fear seeking to control us. Sometimes, it can take days or weeks to work all four components. Yet, they can also happen so quickly that it is hard to tell which came first. No matter how long it takes, however, when all the keys are rooted in a vibrant relationship with the Triune God, incredible results happen.

This may sound like hyperbole, even for many Christian believers. However, if God is as real as we believe, and if God's Spirit was sent to help us, coach us, be with us as the Bible says, then why live life as if we are left on our own to figure things out? Why do we struggle through our daily situations depending exclusively on our own understanding or that of other people? Why don't we stop, center ourselves and ask this personal and loving God for His perspective?

I realize accessing and appreciating the presence of God is no small task. For the majority of us, it is an ability we desperately lack, one that has never been learned nor practiced. However, sensing God's presence and perspective is one skill worth investing in with all of our time and energy. Not only is it the master key to parenting fearlessly, but it yields a peace that is beyond all comprehension, one that ignites a creativity capable of forging new realities.[1]

Now that you at least know where our Source of fearless parenting lies, let's use the keys to unleash a parenting presence you never knew you could have. It all begins with what might seem obvious, but is extremely difficult: recognizing that fear is active.

---

[1] If this kind of relationship sounds inviting but you do not know where to start, do not hesitate to reach out to the LK10 community at LK10.com to sign up for a free Coaching call. This is a global Christian training organization that seeks to see a vibrant family of Jesus within reach of every person on the planet. I have had the joy and privilege of developing their training pathways. We would be delighted in helping equip you to connect heart-to-heart with God and with others.

2
Recognizing Fear

After a couple of deep breaths, I scanned my body and found the pit that had formed in my stomach. Adrenaline was wracking my nervous system. My chest was tight, every breath a hard-fought battle. A few more draughts of air and my emotional pain surfaced. Thinking of my little girl in distress crushed me. Like her, I felt helpless and alone, full of fear.

*****

IF YOU ARE ANYTHING LIKE ME, you may have a hard time understanding what you are feeling at any given moment. Many of us, for different reasons, have been cut off from our feelings for so long that we don't even know they are there, much less what they are. In my case, I was teased as a child for feeling too strongly about things. I apparently "carried my feelings around on my shoulders"…like a "sissy" nonetheless! As a woman trying to excel in the world, I needed to be as level-headed as possible. And if I was passionate about a topic, I was labeled "emotional." I AM NOT EMOTIONAL! (Ahem…)

These are just a few of the cultural-based shaming and destructive messages we face as we seek to build resilience and overcome fear. If we truly want to be fear-free parents, we first must recognize that fear is here. Undoing years of ignoring our feelings, burying them or treating them as absolutes is no small task, but it can be done. Indeed, it must be done.

I picked up a guitar on my own when I was 18. I was not really a musician, but my rhythm was good, and I could play enough chords to lead worship for our college group. I loved playing and singing, so, eventually, I wanted to take guitar lessons to improve my skills.

During my first lesson, the instructor informed me that the way I held my hand for making chords was incorrect, and there was no way I would get better if I did not change the way I played. I was dismayed to learn that I had logged hundreds of hours practicing the wrong form, and that if I wanted to get any better, I would have to retrain my brain to hold my hand differently. The new way was difficult, unnatural and uncomfortable. I left the class depressed as I faced the fact that improving my playing would mean starting from ground zero and relearning everything. Yet, the truth was that the foundation I had laid would only get me as far as I was. If I wanted to play better, I had to start over.

This applies in the realm of emotional maturity as well. Most of us learned to cope with our emotions in ways that have brought us this far in life. Now, however, these same habits are keeping us from growing beyond where we are.

Recognizing Fear

As parents, learning to handle our fear in life-giving ways can only be done through training ourselves in different skills. Recognizing fear involves three micro-skills that give us the self-awareness to perceive the feelings flooding us so that we do not simply react out of them. Instead, we learn to use them to grow and deepen our relationship with ourselves, with God and with others. These three micro-skills are:

- Connecting relationally
- Quieting our thoughts
- Checking in with ourselves

These micro-skills are similar to skills needed to learn a sport or an instrument. Like my stunted guitar playing, many of us have learned to play the "emotional maturity" instrument incorrectly. Therefore, building these new skills is not just about training new habits but unlearning old, unhealthy ones. The only way I could unlearn and relearn new skills was through practice...sheer repetition. Practice doesn't make perfect...until we practice the correct habits.

A WORD ABOUT PRACTICE

Acquiring any skill takes time and practice. We must repeat the drill over and over again, as close to daily as possible, if we want skills to become habits.

When we physically practice something over and over again, it creates muscle memory. Our body learns how to do that activity without us having to think about it. It works for playing guitar, swimming, and even writing. Recognizing our emotions works the same way. The goal is for our body to take over and naturally perform in a skilled way.

Skills are 100% ingrained in muscle memory. I believe this is what Paul had in mind in 1 Timothy 4:7 (NIV):

> *Have nothing to do with godless myths and old wives' tales; rather, train yourself to be godly.*

This Greek verb *gumnazo* means "to train with one's full effort, i.e., with complete physical, emotional force." Imagine an ancient Greek champion preparing for a sporting event.

It is amazing to me that God has designed our bodies, including our brains, to automatically respond in life-giving ways to difficult situations.

Training takes knowing what to practice and what to correct. Thankfully, our brains remain moldable all of our lives, and we can continue to not only learn new skills, but also, with a good coach, correct bad form.

The time to practice the skills we want is *not* in difficult situations when we are overwhelmed or flooding emotionally. No tennis player practices their serve during a match! There is too much pressure and no room for mistakes. Training requires mistakes. The match reveals how much we have or have not practiced. We will be sorely disappointed if we expect to play well without practicing weeks beforehand, focusing on the micro skills for a good serve.

Similarly, a concert is *not* when we should practice our scales. That would be the strangest concert ever! We go to

Recognizing Fear

a piano concert ready to play and/or hear a magnificent composition, not an hour of scale practice. That's even ludicrous to think about!

Skill practice is boring, repetitive and unnatural. It costs us time and attention, emotional and physical effort. The Hebrews author understood this when he wrote:

> *No discipline seems pleasant at the time, but painful. Later on, however, it produces a harvest of righteousness and peace for those who have been trained by it.*
>
> Hebrews 12:11 NIV

Who wouldn't love to see a harvest of righteousness and peace in their family? Yet, we rarely make the connection between righteousness and peace in our relationships, and daily practicing a few boring, repetitive, unnatural exercises. To have mastery when the moment demands, we must practice. We must train. Muscle strength and skills do not come organically or naturally, but only through training.

Tourist to NYC cabbie: "Can you tell me how to get to Carnegie Hall?"

Cabbie: "Practice, practice, practice."

Effective training also requires that we train with others. The skills we are developing are *relational* skills; therefore, a relationship is required to practice them. Start thinking about who would be crazy enough to train with you.

For now, let's break down the three micro-skills we need to master in order to quickly recognize fear:

- Connect relationally
- Quiet our thoughts
- Check in emotionally

CONNECTING RELATIONALLY

According to scientists, our brains can "turn off" or "dim" relationally when we feel overwhelmed. While this defense mechanism might be helpful to shut down pain, it actually thwarts us from sensing our own emotions, showing up for ourselves, and receiving the love or joy we need from another person, at the time we need it the most. When we detach, problems seem bigger, we treat others like objects, and our cravings become monsters.

Christian psychiatrist, Dr. Karl Lehman and neurotheologian, Dr. Jim Wilder, refer to this place in the brain as our "Relational Circuit."[2] Just like an electrical circuit might shut off when it is overloaded, our relational circuit will turn off when we have too much emotion running through our system. Once the circuit blows, we are left without any relational power. Not only do we cease being able to give and receive love around us, we also lose all flexibility and creativity—necessary qualities for problem-solving.

---

[2] For a thorough discussion of the science behind this thinking, I recommend Dr. Karl Lehman's *Outsmarting Yourself.* For a practical application of the science, I refer you to *The Joy Switch* by Chris M Coursey.

The good news is that if we can find that circuit breaker and turn it back on as quickly as possible, we can get relational power flowing again and access the joy and creativity we need to handle difficult situations.

WHEN OUR RELATIONAL CIRCUIT IS ON

Chris Coursey, friend, author, trainer and professional relational coach, calls this circuit breaker "The Joy Switch." In his most recent book, he explains: "The Joy Switch is the lever we must pull, the button we must press to restore the best of our personality, character, and identity...so we become who we always hoped to be" (p. 15).

When we are connected relationally, we have our relational circuit on, and we can see all that is happening around us. We tap into our superpowers, allowing us to use all of our senses to:

- Be flexible (instead of rigid) in our thinking
- Be self-reflective
- Attune to the emotions of ourselves or others
- Use willpower
- Be open and interested in thoughts and feelings
- Regulate emotions
- Find creative solutions
- Focus & shift attention
- Receive joy, care, love, and truth from others

As parents, we need every one of these qualities to train our children well and make the best decisions regarding their future. Without these superpowers, we turn into short-tempered, short-sighted, controlling, irritable, overbearing, absent or addicted shadows of ourselves.

I struggled to stay relational when my children were little. The sheer demand of daily living with three small children in a foreign country with little support structure overwhelmed me regularly. Even though I was working hard to remain relational, at times I would find myself snapping at those I loved or wishing they'd go away.

One day, I called Chris Coursey because I needed help. I thought that after a few years of training, I should be able to stay connected relationally no matter what stress I was under. I felt like a failure that my training was not working.

What Chris told me that day was so freeing. It has helped me over my entire parenting career.

"Toni," Chris said. "The goal of your training is not to avoid a relational shutdown. That is bound to happen no matter how much you can handle. The goal is to recognize when your circuit breaker is blown, and then turn it back on as soon as possible. Don't try to avoid being overwhelmed. It is inevitable. Recognize it and reconnect relationally as soon as possible."[3]

---

[3] In *The Joy Switch,* Coursey goes into detail around how to recognize when our relational circuit is off and how to turn it back on. Incredible resource, complete with helpful exercises you can do with the whole family.

Recognizing Fear

So, how do we recognize that we are "off," and what do we do to turn that joy switch on and get our superpowers back? I will refer you to *The Joy Switch* for in-depth training in this area. Here, I will share briefly what has worked for me.

RECOGNIZING A DISCONNECT

In *The Joy Switch,* Chris shares an excellent checklist that I have used for years to determine whether I am connected relationally or not. I have carried a business card in my wallet with this checklist on it so I can regularly assess if I am disconnected. Answering "yes" to any of these thoughts means your joy switch has blown and your relational circuit is offline.

- ❏ I just want to make a problem, person, or feeling go away.
- ❏ I don't want to listen to what others feel or say.
- ❏ My mind is "locked onto" something upsetting.
- ❏ I don't want to be connected to someone I normally like.
- ❏ I just want to get away, or fight or freeze.
- ❏ I more aggressively interrogate, judge, and fix other people.

In the story of leaving my Anne at school, you can see that my mind was locked onto what was upsetting me.

Once we recognize the disconnect, we must act fast to access our superpowers and face the problem at hand.

RECONNECTING BY PAYING ATTENTION

The quickest way I know to connect relationally with myself is to do a quick scan of my body, paying attention to all it feels.

- *Am I shaking?*
- *Do I want to cry?*
- *Do I want to hit something?*
- *Am I hot or cold?*
- *Am I hungry?*
- *Am I thirsty?*
- *Do I have to use the bathroom?*

This might seem silly, but to answer these questions, I have to relate to myself, thereby turning my relational circuit on. Focusing on what is happening physically is a powerful way to reconnect to ourselves.

Sometimes, however, we need a little more help. Developed by Dr. Jim Wilder, Ed Kouri, and Dr. Karl Lehman, and explained thoroughly in *The Joy Switch*, *Shalom* for my body exercises are a series of three practices to jumpstart the relational part of our brain and restore deep peace—*shalom* to our central nervous system.

As I learned these exercises, I have to admit I felt crazy doing them, even a little embarrassed. However, as I practiced them daily, I became more self-aware of what was going on inside of me. I was also more aware of those around me, including the Divine presence. I could calm my emotions, focus and shift my attention, and realize my options better. It was like having my car jumpstarted in public, slightly embarrassing but effective in getting back on the road and where I needed to go!

In my story, after dropping off Anne at school, I had to stop driving and pull the car over. Taking a few deep breaths, I scanned my body and noticed there was a pit in my stomach. I was shaking the way I do when adrenaline wracks my nervous system. My chest was tight, and I was short of breath. Just noticing these physical sensations connected me relationally and gave me the superpower I needed for the next step of quieting my thoughts.

QUIETING OUR THOUGHTS

My chest was tight, every breath a hard-fought battle. A few more draughts of air and my emotional pain surfaced. Thinking of my little girl in distress crushed me. Like her, I felt helpless and alone, full of fear.

*****

Breathing is the most important factor in learning to quiet our inner world to discern what is going on inside of us, between us and around us. One would think breathing would come naturally considering how often we do it. However, the opposite is true. When we are under stress, we hold our breath, our heart rate speeds up, and if we are not trained to breathe in order to quiet ourselves, what feels natural can quickly lead to a panic attack.

As children, we are often told to hush but never really taught how to quiet ourselves. I have had to learn that as an adult. But the good news is that if I can learn how to quiet, anyone can!

In my first book, *Back to Joy: An Intimate Journey with Jesus into Emotional Health and Maturity,* I share this learning process through journal entries spanning years of practicing the skill of quieting my mind and heart. I recommend that book for more detailed examples of what it looks like to train this micro-skill.

While it does take work to learn to breathe and quiet our thoughts, it is worth it! Dr. Allan Schore, a respected researcher in neuropsychology from UCLA, shares that the inability to down-shift into rest and then up-shift into joy leads to the largest risk of developing a mental illness in a lifetime. His extensive study on attachment and emotional regulation points to this powerful synchronized dance between joy and quiet as the source of all resilience and grit.[4] While we will discuss joy further in the next chapter, simply put, our ability to quiet our internal world through mental rest is the strongest predictor of life-long mental health.

Quieting ourselves allows us to calm the thoughts and emotions that can take our brain and body hostage. Once these racing thoughts are calmed, we can check in with ourselves and be present with all that is stirring, without being held hostage by it.

---

[4] "Attachment, Affect Regulation, and the Developing Right Brain: Linking Developmental Neuroscience to Pediatrics"

Learning to quiet is a physical process; it involves all of your body, not just your mind. We cannot learn to do it by merely reading about it. There are physical ways we can help ourselves quiet mentally so that we can relate better to ourselves and sense that we are not alone. Here are the most helpful activities I have found in learning to quiet myself.

QUIETING ACTIVITIES

The simplest way to practice quiet is...to simply be quiet. For many of us that is easier said than done!

Set your timer to three minutes a day and sit still. Be sensitive to what you notice. This is the easiest way to begin practicing these skills. During this quiet, pay attention to your body, your thoughts and your surroundings.

It often feels like a waste of time for those of us who are used to getting our self-worth from producing, achieving and making things happen. Doing nothing, even for a few minutes, goes against everything Western culture says is important. And yet consistently taking time to sit still is a profound statement that: "the world will not fall apart without me." It affirms that we can cease striving and just be.

Some people focus on their breath, others on their bodies, and others on something in nature. Whatever you focus on, the goal is to be open, meditative, restful and even playful, not solving the world's problems or fixing yourself. You can thank yourself for all the thoughts, urges and feelings that surface, and then invite them to be still and rest. It takes weeks of practice, but eventually the stillness becomes comforting and you can easily increase your practice time.

DEEP BREATHING AND BREATH AWARENESS PRACTICE

Taking a few deep breaths can change everything physiologically. Try it. Stop right now and just breathe deeply three times. What do you notice? How does your body feel differently now?

After a few deep breaths, I typically feel more expansive, my heart rate slows, and my mind becomes clearer. It truly is amazing what simply breathing can do!

Unfortunately, we usually forget to breathe when we are overwhelmed, unless we intentionally practice it, like piano scales or tennis serves. This is where a more intentional breath awareness practice comes in.

When I began practicing silence, I sat for 5 minutes a day and focused on my breath. Once that was comfortable, I increased it to 10 minutes, then 15. If I got distracted, I would return to feeling my breath going in and out of my body. I noticed my thoughts but let them go. Sometimes, I would jot down to-dos that came to mind so that I could return to being aware of my breath without worrying that I would forget something important. [Dr. Dan Siegel's Breath Awareness Practice](#) was extremely helpful to me during that time.

When I began this silence practice (actually recommended by Dallas Willard in *The Spirit of the Disciplines*), some people spoke out against it. Thinking this was New Age, Buddhist or of eastern religion origins; they felt that as Christians, we are to fill our minds, not empty them. My heart still sinks today when I realize some people continue to think this way.

The reality is that we are commanded to "Be still, and know that I [God] am God" (Psalm 46:10). Yet "being still" is a skill that many Christians do not possess. Unfortunately, this black and white thinking is actually prohibiting them from growing the very skill they need to know God.

All of us want to be able to keep our heads about us when crisis hits. The question is: How badly do we want it? And are we willing to train for it? As a new mother, I was desperately tired of being lost in a sea of thoughts and emotions, especially when it came to parenting, so I practiced for years. It has paid off. This skill of quieting is essential if you want to learn to parent without fear and increase your own resilience (as well as your family's resilience).

Yet, quieting our minds is not an end in itself. As Dr. Schore says, it is the "down-shift into rest" and the "up-shift into joy" that trauma-proofs our hearts and minds. Therefore, we quiet so we can check in with our emotions. The checking-in is the beginning of the up-shift to joy—realizing someone is glad to be with us no matter what.

CHECKING-IN EMOTIONALLY

For me, checking-in means noticing my emotions and naming them. Once we name what we are feeling, it allows us to share with others. When someone is glad to be with us no matter what we are feeling, we gain joy strength, our problems seem smaller, and we know we are not alone. But all of that begins by being honest about what we are truly feeling, and for many Christians that is a challenge.

So many of us have been taught that if we trust God, we will not be overwhelmed with fear, anger, sadness, shame or hopeless despair. However, that belief cannot be further from the truth. Trusting is a process that begins with acknowledging present reality. As long as we deny our true emotions, believing we are not *supposed* to feel them, we are defeated before we even begin.

The reality is that when we deny our heavy emotions, they do not go away! Instead, they are allowed to sabotage us by influencing our reactions and keeping us isolated and in pain.

Without even realizing it, I frequently detach from my emotions. My natural response to fear or sadness is to cover it over by being successful on the outside. I switch into task mode, get things done, and look like I have it all together. In my mechanical autopilot, however, I completely lose my relational connection. I come across as a prideful slave driver of myself and those around me. My family tenses up and fears me; they feel guilty for even breathing. Sadly, I used to be completely unaware that this was even happening.

When we look to the Bible for answers, we find a book filled with emotion! The Psalms give us guidance in what to do with our heavier feelings. David modeled brutal honesty with himself and God as he wrote out his "check-ins" in songs or poems. Some people call his heavier works

"Psalms of Disorientation," because David seems confused as he tries to understand how his feelings can be integrated with the truth about himself and God.

In his book, *The Message of the Psalms,* Walter Brueggemann writes on embracing the darkness of life and the heavier Psalms. He explains:

> It's no wonder that the church has intuitively avoided these psalms (of disorientation). They lead us into dangerous acknowledgement of how life really is. They lead us into the presence of God where everything is not polite and civil… They lead us away from the comfortable religious claims of "modernity" in which everything is managed and controlled… The remarkable thing about Israel is that it did not banish or deny the darkness from its religious enterprise. It embraces the darkness as the very stuff of new life. Indeed, Israel seems to know that new life comes nowhere else (p. 53).

Growth comes through times of disorientation. We cannot deny that life is painful, confusing and scary, not if we expect to reach the other side of re-orientation. The only way to integration is through the sea of emotion.

Whenever I tell people that their feelings are valid and vital, someone invariably responds, "Yes, but we can't live by our feelings. We have to live by faith."

My heart sinks every time I hear that statement. I know it is borne of a desire to help and protect. Yet, I also understand that people are concerned that we will make decisions based on our feelings instead of a sense of morality and truth. Many believe that acknowledging and understanding our feelings lead to letting them control us. Ironically, the opposite is actually true.

To *not* live by our feelings, we actually have to see them as valid and important so that we can disarm them! Otherwise, they will continue causing unwelcome reactions in us. Naming our feelings allows us to interact with them and then respond in healthy ways.

In LK10, the Christian leadership organization I train with, we give people a model for training themselves relationally. We invite all of our leaders to find one or two other people who will commit to practice these skills with them, as close to daily as possible. Because we are practicing connecting heart-to-heart with each other and with the Divine, we call this model a Church of Two (CO2), or a Church of Few.

Naming this gathering "church" is intentional. We want people to understand that being the people of God—being His Church—is all about heart-to-heart connection with each other and with God, not about programs, buildings, dos and don'ts. We also want people to understand that church has to be practiced daily in our most intimate relationships if we expect to be church in larger contexts.

In our Church of Two, we share two simple rhythms that are the same as what I'm proposing here: checking in and listening to God. As couples, friends and families learn to share their feelings with each other, learning to *be glad to be together no matter what,* joy is experienced and resilience grows. As we learn to listen to God together and perceive that He is glad to be with us **no matter what**, fear dissipates and our creativity to solve problems is unleashed. (More on listening in the next few chapters.)

Our first practice: checking in, is incredibly simple but not easy. In some circumstances, it might not even be safe. Sometimes, we share what we are feeling only to have someone tell us why we should not feel that way. Maybe they are uncomfortable with our emotions and react by trying to teach us something they think will help. Worse, they may make fun of us. That is why it is important to have someone to practice with who will handle your emotions with great care, someone who will listen and be glad to be with you without needing to change you, fix you or correct you.

As you will see in the following chapters, there is time for correction and helping, but that can only come once we feel seen, validated, attuned to and loved.

As the model parent, God cares for us. He wants us to share our hearts with Him and with those around us. He designed us for joy.[5] Our feelings are the windows to our souls. Heart-to-heart connection with each other and with God is the goal. However, we cannot be known or deeply know others if we are hiding, denying or suppressing our feelings. It is through acknowledging them that we grow the joy strength to overcome all obstacles.

Acknowledging our feelings takes practice.

---

[5] See *Joy Fueled: Catalyzing a Revolution of Joyful Communities* by Toni M Daniels, Dr. Kent Smith and John C White.

Parenting yourself well means recognizing when fear is active. If you were not trained in these matters of the heart as a child, God wants to train you, re-parent you and show you not only how to become resilient yourself, but also how to build a joy-fueled, resilient family. The micro-skills of connecting relationally, quieting our thoughts and checking-in with our feelings are essential parts of recognizing when fear is here.

When I realized that my bad form on the guitar was holding me back, I felt quite discouraged with the work ahead of me to correct the bad habits I had learned and build new ones. This discouragement felt overwhelming, and I avoided playing guitar for a long time. In fact, I never did retrain my brain. I had no one to train with. I decided that my level of expertise was sufficient for my purposes.

If our emotions are overwhelming, we will avoid facing them for fear of getting lost in them, and we settle for less than all God has for us. This is why a Church of Two is so important to the practices I recommend. Perhaps if I had had a guitar partner to practice with me, I may have never given up. In sharing together and sensing God's presence, we gain joy strength to train well. We not only train in learning to recognize our fear, but we also learn to wield the second key to dismantling fear: realizing we are not alone.

3

Realizing You Are Not Alone

He drew me closer, face to face, kneeling in front of me, cupping my cheeks in his hands. I looked up, his face filled with compassion. He felt my anguish. He was not afraid of my feelings or situation. He was glad to be with me. I was not alone.

*****

And I will ask the Father, and He will give you another Helper (Comforter, Advocate, Intercessor—Counselor, Strengthener, Standby), to be with you forever— the Spirit of Truth, whom the world cannot receive [and take to its heart] because it does not see Him or know Him, but you know Him because He (the Holy Spirit) remains with you continually and will be in you.

John 14:16-17 (AMP)

> *I will not leave you as orphans [comfortless, bereaved, and helpless]; I will come [back] to you.*
>
> John 14:18 (AMP)

*****

We are never alone; not ever! God has promised us His very life-presence always, and not just near us, but in our "innermost being." Those are strong words, even strange words for many, but they are true words. Unfortunately, even though God is near, we often cannot sense Him with us. There could be many reasons for this.

- We are not connected relationally.
- Our relational circuit is blown.
- We do not know how to quiet.
- We do not know our own feelings enough to distinguish God's presence within us from our own thoughts.

There may even be a dismissive tendency hard-wired into our brain that keeps us from recognizing God's presence consistently. But just because we do not recognize Immanuel, *God with us,* does not mean He is not here.

It breaks my heart that so many Christians think the spiritual life is one of intellectual ideas we must ascent to. They are satisfied with memorizing Bible verses, studying scripture, singing songs and listening to sermons, believing that in these activities they will find character transformation. When in actuality, it is only in the context of relationship where we find character development.

Don't get me wrong. Theology, the study of the Bible, and good teaching are very real components of our life together as Christians, and I am grateful for having enjoyed some of the best while growing up. However, as Wilder and Hendricks explain in *The Other Half of Church*, our character is *not* transformed by information, correct thinking and good choices (p. 47). These activities only appeal to the left side of our brain, which is actually *not* the part of our brain that controls our behavior. It is in the other half of our brain, the right side, where our emotions, experiences, and relational attachment are lodged that shapes our character.

The New Testament speaks of this relational component over and over again. What do all of these verses have in common?

> *But I tell you the truth, it is to your advantage that I go away; for if I do not go away, the Helper (Comforter, Advocate, Intercessor—Counselor, Strengthener, Standby) will not come to you; but if I go, I will send Him (the Holy Spirit) to you [to be in close fellowship with you].*
>
> John 16:7 (AMP)
>
> *He who believes in Me [who adheres to, trusts in, and relies on Me], as the Scripture has said, 'From his innermost being will flow continually rivers of living water.' But He was speaking of the [Holy] Spirit, whom*

those who believed in Him [as Savior] were to receive afterward. The Spirit had not yet been given, because Jesus was not yet glorified (raised to honor).

John 7:38-39 (AMP)

May He grant you out of the riches of His glory, to be strengthened and spiritually energized with power through His Spirit in your inner self, [indwelling your innermost being and personality].

Ephesians 3:16 (AMP)

In the same way the Spirit [comes to us and] helps us in our weakness. We do not know what prayer to offer or how to offer it as we should, but the Spirit Himself [knows our need and at the right time] intercedes on our behalf with sighs and groanings too deep for words.

Romans 8:26

Casting all your cares [all your anxieties, all your worries, and all your concerns, once and for all] on Him, for He cares about you [with deepest affection, and watches over you very carefully].

1 Peter 5:7 (AMP)

All of these verses point to the part of the Trinity Jesus called the "Spirit" who would come to us, comfort us, be glad to be with us, care for us, guide us, intercede for us, and on and on. It is a promise of God with us and within us, Immanuel, enjoying us no matter what.

Joy is that feeling we get when someone is glad to be with us no matter what. It, not information, is the very foundation of a securely bonded relationship. Let me say that again, joy, not information, is the foundation of a securely bonded relationship. And when we have a secure relational bond with God and others, our character grows and changes. Information alone cannot do that. When a brain is in low joy, all kinds of addictions and personality disorders can take over, regardless of what intellectual truth or theology a person mentally assents to.

So, if a secure, joy bond is crucial, how do we cultivate it? When we are infants, we form an emotional attachment to our parents before we know anything about them. It is based on non-verbal, non-intellectual activity such as smiling, laughing, feeding, snuggling, receiving, and getting our needs met before we ask. If our parents see our needs and attune to our emotions (more on attunement in the second part of this book), we form healthy attachment. If we are to form a healthy bond with God, it will involve non-verbal, non-intellectual time with Him, receiving from Him and letting Him attune to our needs and emotions until we feel "felt." Perhaps this is what Jesus meant when He said:

> *Truly I say to you, unless you turn and become like children, you will never enter the kingdom of heaven.*
>
> Matthew 18:3

This is why LK10 recommends forming a church of two. After checking in, we practice listening to God together (as close to daily as possible). We take three to five minutes in silence and ask God "How do you feel about being with us today?" Then, during the silence, we pay attention or, using Dr. Siegel's acronym, we SIFT our minds for any spontaneous Sensations, Images, Feelings or Thoughts.

This question, "How do you feel about being with us today?" protects us from our own transactional tendencies with ourselves and God. It cuts straight to the heart of our identity.

- Am I lovable?
- Am I enjoyable?
- Is it okay to feel the way I feel?
- Does God "get" me or am I too much to handle?
- Does God still want to be with me even though I am struggling and not living up to my own expectations?

So often we are struggling to solve a problem intellectually.

- How do I get my child to clean their room?
- Why can't I figure out how to get my kids to stop fighting?
- How do I respond to my child cutting themselves?
- Where will the money come from this month to pay the bills?

- Should I homeschool or send my kids to public or private school?
- Am I the reason my child turned to drugs?
- Why can't I get out of bed earlier to spend time with myself and God?

All of these are valid concerns, and it is beautiful to go to our Source of Life for the solutions. However, connecting on a heart-to-heart level *with ourselves and God* is absolutely essential *before* we solve problems and make decisions...especially when fear is involved. Fear distorts reality and hinders us from creating new solutions. It keeps us in a reactionary, protective stance, unable to assess risk or freely consider options.

Wilder and Hendricks remind us that when we can sense that God is happy to be with us and is smiling at us, this joy naturally removes fear from the relationship. A goal we are invited to have "in our bond with God is to nurture a loving relationship until it has no fear" (p. 61). As we read in 1 John 4:18 (AMP):

> *There is no fear in love [dread does not exist]. But perfect (complete, full-grown) love drives out fear.*

If information, correct thinking and good choices are all our Christian life consists of, we are missing the very purpose of scripture itself: to lead us into a vibrant relationship with the Living God where we can see Him smiling at us, where His Spirit is closer than our breath, guiding, coaching, comforting, interceding, counseling and strengthening us from *within*. This is the foundation of all character change. It is from this inner place of joy that truth can be received and creativity can flow.

The solution to our problems is often that we need to get unstuck emotionally and get back to joy. We desperately want to know what to do to solve our problems, but first we need to viscerally know and experience that we are not alone and that we are loved no matter what.

It is out of this safe, intimate space that "rivers of living water flow." Asking God: "How do you feel about being with me today?" reminds us to start with the relational aspect of our problem. Then, move on to asking God, "What do you want me to know about the problem at hand?"

How do we cultivate this inner life with God's presence? What does it look like practically speaking?

From my story of dropping off Anne at pre-school (Chapter 1), in those few short seconds in the car, recognizing fear was active, I connected relationally, quieted myself and checked in. It was obvious I needed the Comforter and Counselor. And because I have been practicing listening to God daily for over 10 years, I could sense God's presence tangibly with me. Thankfully, on that day, my mind and body automatically turned to righteousness and peace. I sought my secure attachment with Jesus by anchoring myself into my appreciation memory on the beach where I have seen His face smiling over me before. There, I could quickly interact with Him, share my feelings and sense how He felt about being with me.

ANCHORING IN APPRECIATION

A good friend of mine and co-author of *Joyful Journey: Listening to Immanuel,* John Loppnow, likes to say that "appreciation is the passcode into the presence of God" (p. 15). I have indeed found this to be true. When our minds are focused on the problems around us, it is difficult to sense that God is near. In fact, the problems surround us and hide the Divine from us. The Psalmist knew what he was talking about when he said "Enter his gates with thanksgiving in your hearts" (Psalm 100).

While there are many ways to sense God's presence, appreciation is our secret weapon. When we remember moments of gratitude, peace, safety and awe, we flood our bodies with endorphins and the relationships around us become larger and closer than the problems. It is like taking a mini-vacation where you allow all the good to enter your soul, causing your body to feel expansive, taller, buoyant, resilient.

Sometimes my appreciation memories are from my childhood, like the time I was doing art outside. I was probably 10 years old. It was a hot day. I was lying on the cool concrete, tummy down, painting a watercolor picture of a tree. I felt at peace. Time stopped. There was nowhere else but there, no worries at all. I felt connected to myself and to nature. I enjoyed myself, enjoyed painting and admiring nature. I felt deep inner peace.

Other times, my appreciation memories are ones that only exists in my mind. Places my imagination invents where I find myself in different ages and forms, and I sense God's presence with me. Some people might call these "safe" places. When I go there, I immediately feel everything associated with them.

There is the beach, for example, where Jesus has carried me for miles. It is a place where He has prepares formal dinners for me, watches me build sand castles on the shore, and enjoys just being with me. He comforts me, confronts me, quiets me, coaches me and holds me like a father while we watch the sunset. I am always an adult when I go there.

Another safe place is a field of yellow flowers and I am 8 years old. The weather is always the perfect temperature, the flowers always in bloom. There are kaleidoscopes of butterflies, and I am delighted to be there. The field is surrounded by scary woods, but Jesus has shown me that the wolves do not come into the light. I am safe in the field. And if I go into the woods, I go because He is leading me there. As long as I stay close to Him, I am safe because light emanates from His very being.

This field of flowers is a place just for me to receive from Him all that I need: safety, instruction and coaching about my personality, design and calling. When I am there, I do not have to carry anyone else's burdens. I get to rest and feel precious and playful.

These imaginative spaces came to me early in adulthood but have developed over the 20 years of interacting with God there. As you can see, we can build appreciation with real memories or "safe places". Searching for these appreciative, fully-alive memories and sharing them with others builds belonging and resilience.

Collecting such memories also prepares our brains to find them in times of need, as I did that day in the car after dropping off Anne. Collecting appreciation memories instead of information is a whole-brained activity involving all of our heart and mind. This is a very practical way to live out Philippians 4 where Paul commands us:

> *Whatever is true, whatever is honorable and worthy of respect, whatever is right and confirmed by God's word, whatever is pure and wholesome, whatever is lovely and brings peace, whatever is admirable and of good repute; if there is any excellence, if there is anything worthy of praise, think continually on these things [center your mind on them, and implant them in your heart].*
>
> Philippians 4:8 AMP

The Greek that is translated "think continually on these things" really means "collect" such things. Many people have taken this verse to mean we should memorize more scripture. However, again, if we are doing so without engaging our relational brain, it will not bring about true character change, nor will it necessarily help us sense God physically with us when we need Him the most.

What if collecting our appreciation memories really was the passcode into the presence of God, unleashing the very power of heaven in our hearts and minds, helping us form strong, joy-based attachment bonds with Jesus? Why would we not do that? Because it takes practice. And many of us do not have a space in our lives or community with which to practice these sorts of things.

Finding my appreciation memories has not always been this automatic for me. In *Back to Joy: An Intimate Journey with Jesus into Emotional Health and Maturity*, I share my personal journal entries during the first 18 years of learning these skills and collecting my memories. You will find companionship there for beginning your journey of learning to recognize your emotions and realizing you are not alone.

I have included here in this book, in the Resources section, an appreciation log where you can begin your collection. It includes a video from my husband, Matt, demonstrating how to use the log. Feel free to print one out for every day and use it to prompt your reflections.

In LK10, we not only practice daily with at least one other person, called our Church of Two partner, but we also have communities of practice where we gather for the sole purpose of practicing all the skills I'm sharing here. It is often hard to find others willing to practice relational training. And yet training by yourself is rarely effective, especially when you are working towards a secure attachment with God, who often reveal Himself through community. Do not hesitate to reach out to www.LK10.com to begin your training with other like-minded believers.

*****

Besieged with utter fear and despair in the car after leaving Anne at school, desperate for help, I did not quote a scripture to myself. I did not try to use words to calm my soul. I did not simply tell myself over and over again that God was with me, hoping in vain that my emotions would respond. No, in seconds I went to my safe place on the beach where Jesus waits for me in my innermost being. Seeing Him in my imagination as He knelt to gently touch my shoulder, I instantly *felt* not alone. There was safe space to experience all of my feelings. His eyes were a sea of peace, love and grace. I was protected and contained, no matter how strong the emotions grew; He was glad to be with me even if I was overwhelmed with fear.

This joy—that Jesus is glad to be with me no matter what—allowed me to unravel the tsunami of emotions wracking my body and not get lost in them. He was there to contain me and pull me out of wherever I was heading emotionally. Recognizing my fear and realizing I was not alone grounded me in a real relationship, one that I could see and feel. Only then, as I was held by the gaze of my loving God, did the transformative, truth-telling conversation begin. The question, "What is it you would like me to know?" opened a floodgate to the third component of dismantling fear, that of receiving truth.

4
Receiving Truth

"What do I need to know?" I pleaded as he lovingly held my gaze.

"Toni, my child, do you believe I am bigger than this?"

"Yes, yes, yes," I sobbed. "Of course, You are bigger than any mistake I can make. Of course, You are bigger than any brokenness that seeks to harm Anne. Yes, yes, yes."

With every yes, I felt despair leave, loneliness dissipate and fear subside. With every yes, I received Truth, letting in a little more of Him each time.

The truth was, I was not alone. He was with me, and He was bigger than my fear. He was also with Anne. He could heal any wound she suffered. Trust filled my soul and fear had no space left to cling to. Alone in my car, I rested with Jesus, collapsing into His arms. Safely held by Truth, my heart rate slowed and my mind quieted.

*****

RECEIVING TRUTH WITH YOUR HEART

Once you recognize fear is active and that you are not alone, the component to dismantling the fear is that of receiving truth, both the One who *is* Truth and His perspective of reality—His truth. Truth is not just right-thinking; it is a person: Jesus. He is the Way, the Truth, and the Life (ref. John 14:6).

Receiving the person of Christ is so much more than giving mental assent to an idea or a concept. When I receive an idea, *I* am still in control. I can decide what to do with that idea and how far to let it change me. With an idea such as a theological concept, I can know about God, feel secure in my belief and even think that therein lies salvation, yet I can do all of this without actually knowing the Divine as God with me—without letting this powerful presence into me to challenge all that I think is true.

When Jesus was physically present on earth, this was His criticism of the God-followers of His day,

> *You study the Scriptures diligently because you think that in them you have eternal life. These are the very Scriptures that testify about me, yet you refuse to come to me to have life.*
>
> John 5:39-40 NIV

Letting Truth with a capital "T"—Jesus Himself—into my heart, mind, body and soul, always feels risky and vulnerable. I never know what He is going to do or say. He reveals all, even the hidden parts of me that I don't even fully understand. In seconds, I could be overwhelmed with love and undone with conviction about wrong beliefs I did not know I had. Or, I could be flooded with grief as He takes me to a traumatic memory He would like to heal.

Not knowing where this is going can feel disorienting, but the Guide is trustworthy. Through practicing over and over again, asking God: "What do I need to know?" and saying *yes* to the Truth, Jesus and His perspective, the Way unfolds before me and the Life and Light are my guides. The more we practice, the more trust we build.

I have also found that listening is not only about paying attention to my own thoughts but also to the nonverbal activity happening in my appreciation memories. As you can see in the above story, Jesus communicated nonverbally through facial expressions, gestures, and body movements. He knelt in front of me, gently touched my shoulder, showed empathy in His face and held my gaze. Many times, we do not notice what He is saying because we cannot see Him in our imagination, or we simply do not know how to pay attention or how to be aware of what is happening.

Apart from images of Jesus interacting in our imagination, we can also sense God's presence through spontaneous sensations, feelings, and thoughts. When Dr. Dan Siegel teaches awareness, he says we are to SIFT our minds, paying attention to Sensations, Images, Feelings and Thoughts (SIFT). As any of these spontaneously arise, we could be perceiving the presence of God.

Connecting heart-to-heart with God looks different for each person and can look very different each time you practice it. Going to an appreciation memory, visually finding God's presence there, sharing my heart with my Creator and asking the two questions "How do you feel about being with me? What do I need to know?" is my go-to practice for receiving the Truth—Jesus and His perspective—into the core of my being.

The truth that God can heal any wound we might suffer is a hard reality to grasp but powerful in dismantling fear. In fact, I have sensed God say this to me over and over again in a variety of situations. The most powerful moment was in 2014 after I had been physically attacked and robbed in front of my house in Uruguay, South America. The next day, I took some time to process the trauma using the four Rs: Recognizing, Realizing, Receiving, and Responding. I recognized fear was active by connecting relationally, quieting and checking in. Then, by nestling myself into an appreciation moment of watching my children play together, I realized I was not alone. My heart swelled with gratefulness and joy. They were so precious to me.

In that moment, I sensed God say, "I feel about you the same way you feel about your children, Toni. You are my precious one."

This is where the interactive receiving of Truth began.

"But, Lord," I argued, "I would never let my children suffer if I could stop it. And yet, you let me suffer at the hands of robbers."

I touched the bruises on my face and rub burns on my neck from where I had been slammed into the car and the purse ripped from my body.

"I did stop it," Jesus replied, confusing me even more. "That is what the cross was all about."

"But you didn't stop it last night." I began to build my case. "They could have done so much worse, and you would not have stopped it. You don't stop the suffering. Your people suffer horrendous things at the hands of cruel people all the time! Innocent people suffer more than I can understand. What difference does the cross make now, in this world?"

I was begging for answers, and not cute Sunday School answers telling me to just trust. I needed a Truth that could make sense of my experience, one I could lead from. The next day was Good Friday, and I was responsible for the message for our people. What was I to share?

Jesus reached out for me, "Your heart does not have to stay wounded. I can heal you now. I want to heal you now. Come to me."

His invitation was convincing. I knew His healing touch. Giving up my anger, I ran to Him.

With me in His arms, He pulled back, showed me His hands and continued, "I know it hurts. I know it hurts when someone hurts you, and you don't deserve it."

His scars reminded me of His suffering here on earth.

"How do you heal me?" I asked gently.

"I have your heart safe inside me. They can hurt your body but they can never take you away from me. You are mine!"

Not convinced, I protested in my fear, "But where were you last night?"

I immediately got an image of how God was all around me during the attack—Father, Son and Spirit.

"I was all around you, surrounding you. They cannot take what is mine. It is safely hidden in me. You are safely hidden in me. Do not fear. I could stay relational on the cross because I did not fear what they were doing to me. I did not fear because I knew that nothing was beyond my healing. Nothing, nothing, nothing is beyond my healing."

He paused to search my heart to see if I got what he was saying.

"Do you believe me?" He continued. "Not torture, not rape, not child abuse, not murder...nothing!"

While I appreciated the truth He was trying to help me grasp, my mind returned to the physical pain I was in and how much worse it could have been. I responded, "But these things hurt so badly."

"Yes," he agreed with me, showing me His hands. "They hurt, but they are not to be feared because they can be healed! The only way to overcome fear is to know beyond a shadow of a doubt that I can and will redeem, restore, and repair ALL that has been broken, abused, hurt, lost."

What happened next was like nothing I had ever encountered before or since. I felt transported to a different dimension where I could see the restoration of all things. Every person, every crime, every hurt, every abuse, every atrocity...undone, healed, restored, redeemed. I cannot put to words the images, feelings or sensations. This was not just something Jesus was telling me; He was showing me. My whole body was flooded with awe, amazement and hope. The image felt so real that I physically remember throwing myself to my knees in worship of Him and begging Him to come: *Thy Kingdom come, thy will be done on earth as it is in heaven.*

This experience was so powerful that my perspective has been forever altered. Fear, while it sometimes raises its head, is easily disseminated in the presence of this image, this vision. The truth radiates from within me.

I still hate the suffering and pain we go through and our children go through. I am angry and grief-stricken over the hurt in the world. Sadness, grief and sometimes anger are appropriate emotions and my companions. But fear is insidious. It keeps us from boldly living the relational Truth that is the resurrected Jesus Christ.

And while I would love to help every person see this reality I see, my declaring truth is not going to be very helpful to you. You need to hear Jesus speak truth over you in *your* deepest fear. My hope is that the stories I share will inspire you to seek that Truth for yourself.

It is my firm belief that God wants to give all of us this "knowing" to the core of our being. I can tell you to "not fear" and "trust God," or I can guide you into the very presence of Truth Himself and have you experience what it looks and feels like to not fear. Only then does trust flow out of that deep experience from within. Instead of a feeble attempt to suppress the fear, deny it or medicate it because you believe you are not supposed to be afraid, you have the option to experience the One who removes all fear.

In the skills guide at the end of the book, you will find other resources that have been helpful in cultivating this kind of relationship with God, where He is on the inside parenting us, so to speak, and leading us out of fear and into truth.

DISCERNING

Listening to God and sensing His presence take practice, and the results always need to be evaluated in community. However, the discerning needs to happen *after* the listening time is over, not during it! The quickest way to get your brain out of relational mode and thwart your ability to sense God is by getting into a debate with yourself around whether what you are experiencing or hearing is really from God.

During the listening time, if I get distracted wondering if what I am sensing is from God or not, I simply thank my analytical brain for trying to protect me from being led astray. Then I ask it to rest, assuring myself that I will analyze the content after I have finished listening.

In LK10, we believe that this discerning is best done in community. We share with our Church of Two (CO2) and other CO2s what we experience and what message we take away from that experience. Our community then helps us discern whether what we are hearing sounds like God to them. And many times we hear God through them as well.

We use three questions for discerning:

1. Is it congruent with Scripture?
2. Is it congruent with the community's experience of God? Does that sound like God to them?
3. Does it produce the fruit of the spirit (love, joy, peace, etc.) in my innermost being?

Having these three ways to measure what we are sensing helps protect and guide us. The more we practice and have confirmed that what we are hearing sounds like God, the more confidence we acquire. Let's look in detail at these three qualifiers.

IS IT CONGRUENT WITH SCRIPTURE?

From the beginning of creation, we see a Triune God speaking among themselves, "Let us make man in our image, after our likeness" (Genesis 1:26). Over 2000 times in the Old Testament there are phrases such as, "And God spoke to Moses" or "the word of the Lord came to Jonah" or "God said."

As it turns out, our God is quite conversational. During the birth of Jesus, God spoke to Mary through an angel. He spoke to Joseph through a dream. He spoke to the shepherds through an angel. And He spoke to the Magi through their own hearts, leading them to the young Jesus and then, through a dream, directing their safe departure.

During His life, Jesus modeled a life of constant interaction with God the Father, saying,

> *The Son can do nothing by himself; he can do only what he sees his Father doing, because whatever the Father does the Son also does.*
>
> John 5:19

After His death and resurrection, Jesus sent the Spirit of Truth to be with us and to guide us into all truth (ref. John 16:13). And we see modeled time after time how the early Christians were led, guided and comforted by God's tangible presence among them.

Scripture guides not only our doctrine but also our practice. As we hear truth, we judge it against the measuring rod of the Bible. These sacred scriptures tell us who our God is, what He does and why He does it. As we receive Truth, through sensations, images, feelings, thoughts, nature, dreams, etc., we should compare them to these sacred writings to determine if, indeed, what we are experiencing is congruent with the truth we find there.

IS IT CONGRUENT WITH OUR PEOPLE'S EXPERIENCE OF GOD?

In my lifetime of practicing listening and sensing God's presence, it is like God to attune to me, meaning He validates my emotions, sees me, and is glad to be with me no matter what. (More on attunement in Chapter 6.)

Once I feel this Divine joy and delight over me, God challenges my faulty thinking…about God's nature, myself, and the situation at hand. The Trinity's perspective tends to completely dismantle the fear or shame that was holding me hostage and keeping me from seeing a way forward.

With my emotions at peace and my perspective transformed to what Jesus sees, a creativity like no other is unleashed, and I am ready to respond to the problem at hand. God invites me into co-creating new solutions together. This is the mysterious collaboration that not only dismantles our fears, but builds resilience in our families as well.

As we share with others how God communicates with us, they give testimony of their own experience of God. If someone is hearing things that are not within the community's experience, we wonder together about those things, hold them lightly and wait and see what God reveals corporately.

DOES IT PRODUCE THE FRUIT OF THE SPIRIT IN MY INNERMOST BEING?

> *But the fruit of the Spirit [the result of His presence within us] is love [unselfish concern for others], joy, [inner] peace, patience [not the ability to wait, but how we act while waiting], kindness, goodness, faithfulness, gentleness, and self-control.*
>
> Galatians 5:22-23 AMP

Whenever we sense God's presence holding us, loving us, enjoying us, confronting us, challenging us and encouraging us, it always produces the fruit of the Spirit.

This fruit is the signature of God, proof of the Spirit's presence.

Sometimes I refer to this as an emotional shift towards love, joy and peace because that is exactly the way I experience it. In any given moment, I can come to God angry, sad, discouraged or afraid, but after time with the Trinity, an emotional shift happens. My body, mind and soul are filled with peace. I may not have answers to the problem. My circumstances might be the same, and yet God has brought truth in such a way that causes a very real emotional and physical shift within me, one that allows the Spirit to bear fruit in me.

If what we hear or sense from God does not lead to love, joy, peace, patience, kindness, goodness, gentleness and self-control, then there is sufficient doubt that it is God we are hearing. This is why we practice listening to God together and as close to daily as possible. Discerning takes practice.

Amazingly so, during this three-step process of 1. Recognizing fear is active, 2. Realizing I am not alone, and 3. Receiving Truth, God is parenting me and modeling for me how to show up as a parent in the lives of my own children. Sometimes that is all that happens. My perspective changes, I am filled with the fruit of the Spirit and I go on. However, other times God does not stop there. Sometimes, God invites me to respond to the situation at hand by co-creating new realities that build resilience in my own family.

5

Responding By Co-creating New Realities

In the quiet, I sensed Jesus reply with very direct advice. "Spend time alone with just her each day. While Matt naps, give your full attention to her. Play with her, whatever she wants to play. Watch her and just be with her...and don't worry about her at school. I, Myself, will comfort her there. Wait and see what happens over the next few days. If you don't see things getting better, we can talk about it again."

*****

God had attuned to my heart, soothed my fears, and had given me a simple parenting plan that was exactly what Anne needed. I would never have imagined this creative solution on my own. I was now able to respond to this whole situation by co-creating a new reality with the Divine—my Parent, my Coach, and the One who knows Anne's soul better than I do.

The results were amazing. Anne adjusted within a few days. Her teacher noticed, and I had the opportunity to share all that God was doing. Sharing is easier when the demonstration happens right in front of a person.

As we do the work of dismantling our fears, new options come, a new way of seeing the same situation arises, a plan for how to handle the situation forms. These are moments of co-creating with the Divine. They do not always lead to immediate resolution; however, these new realities give us stability in the midst of the storm and an internal peace that radiates to those around us, including our children. Many times, finding peace for ourselves is most of the battle.

This was no more evident than what happened next with Anne a few months after she had adjusted to being in school. She began randomly screaming at me every time she saw me. I had no idea why. After several days of it, my heart was broken. I decided to take a morning away to share with the Trinity and ask them what to do. What ensued blew me away.

I began by trying to recognize what I was feeling. I shared with Papa God how my heart was in pain and how confused I was.

I then tried to realize I was not alone by finding an appreciation memory where I could sense the Spirit of God with me. We were purchasing a retreat center and the funding campaign was focused on sharing amazing stories of gratitude with the people who funded our work. I felt amazed at God for growing our faith. I felt provided for as well as thrilled to be a part of something so much bigger than myself. Tension left my shoulders and an unburdening began.

Responding by Co-creating New Realities

In this space of gratitude, grief surfaced and an overwhelming feeling threatened to settle in. I did my relational circuit exercises again and breathed deeply. Life had been so hard that month. Living in a foreign country with a 12-year-old and two toddlers with little family support was difficult. To make matters worse, the garage regularly flooded with sewage, the kitchen sink was leaking, a valve in the bathroom broke, our electricity to our dishwasher and water heater failed, I had an ear infection and people on our Christian work team were struggling to get along.

I was definitely overwhelmed. As I took several deep breaths, I sensed Jesus close. I remembered a memory where He was glad to be with me even when I was tired. He knew how hard life was, and He wanted to give me energy to get through what I was facing.

"I'm here, my child," I heard Jesus whisper close to me. "Just breathe and be with me."

I continued breathing deeply while sensing Jesus right in front of me. As I inhaled, He exhaled life and energy into me. I rested in that life-giving space. Then my heart poured out.

"I want to live in a light, emotional land, not a heavy land. I want to be a safe harbor for my children. But instead, I feel like they're afraid of me! At least Annie seems to be. Whenever I walk in the room she screams. This has never happened before! We had the most precious relationship for the first 18 months of her life. And then several unexpected things happened that I fear have affected her to the point of changing her identity. Namely, we had four moves in six months, and I was separated from her for several weeks when her premature brother was born. I feel like I have been trying to regain our relationship ever since. I had no idea of the emotional damage all of this would do to her. I am so sorry."

As the words came, tears flowed.

"What would you like me to know about Annie?" I asked between sobs.

Jesus' face was soft. He was sitting right in front of me, not just in a memory, but I sensed Him with me sitting on the coffee table. I could not visually see Him, but nearly so. I felt Him so present, as good as tangible.

Sitting knee to knee with me, He began, "What is done, is done, my child. You cannot undo it. But I will redeem it in her life. Do not fear. I will restore her to you."

Fear! I did not realize I was afraid. I love Anne so much. She is so beautiful!

"What am I afraid of?" I asked Jesus and myself. "What kind of fear is here?"

My own heart replied, "Fear that she has been damaged by being away from me those months I was in the hospital. Fear that that experience at such a young age changed her whole personality. Fear that her true heart is now buried under fear, and that it might not ever come back. I am afraid that we will have conflict always and that raising her will be full of grief and strife. Anne holds grudges. I am afraid I have lost her and that the rest of her life is going to be very hard."

As each fear emerged, tears of grief claimed my face. I felt it in my gut. I was almost nauseous. Fear of losing someone you love is a deep attachment pain that can even alter the way we see reality.

Jesus leaned forward, wiped tears from my eyes and began His truth telling.

"I have a plan for Anne. You must trust this process. Stay with me on this. She is her own person. Let her differentiate from you. Your job is to love her no matter what, to see her as I see her, and to take good care of yourself in the relationship."

His words were weighty; His eyes sincere.

I was overtaken with the need to give her back to him. I wanted to trust him with her.

"I give her to you, my Lord. She was my Anne Elizabeth, my 'gift of God's abundant grace.' She was so precious and so perfect. I give my Grace back to you. I have hurt her, life has hurt her, and she needs your healing, Father. Please heal her."

As I said this, memories came of holding my little Anne as a baby. I pictured her swaddled in my arms. She was the quietest, most observant baby I had ever known. She rarely cried, and she brought much healing to my soul after having had a child who cried quite frequently.

I looked at Jesus, and the idea came to me to hand my little baby over to him. I wanted to physically give her to him. I handed this little bundle in my memory to the Healer of Hearts. He took her into His arms.

I already felt emotionally lighter as I thanked Him for taking the weight of her health onto Himself. I could carry it no more.

Then, He took her and enveloped her into His own body and I sensed Him say to me, "I am hiding her in myself as a baby before the trauma even began. I will keep her safe. And I will integrate her when the time is right. You can trust me to do this."

There was my Anne, before the trauma, whole, healthy, and now hidden. Hidden in Christ until the time when she would be revealed.

While that felt incredibly comforting and promising, my heart realized this could take a lifetime. I found myself blurting out loud, "I don't want to have to wait 20 years!"

He chuckled and assured me it would not take that long.

My fear was completely gone. I realized that nothing was beyond Jesus' repair. I left my room fully expecting to walk into the kitchen and have Anne scream when I entered the room, and I was OK with that. There was a deep peace flowing through me.

Then, the most amazing thing happened. As I entered the kitchen, Anne looked up and made eye contact with me and smiled. Taken aback, I glanced over at my husband, wondering could this really be possible? I walked over to Anne and placed my hand on her shoulders. She scooted over for me to sit next to her. It was as if God had already done the work of integrating her!

Responding by Co-creating New Realities

I still can't help but wonder if she had merely been reflecting the fear that she had seen inside of me. So much can be passed through eye contact, whether I'm at peace or full of fear. I realize how important it is for me to dismantle my own fear so that I can radiate peace to those around me.

*****

The way toward building resilience within our families flows out of the work we do to recognize our fear, realize we are not alone, receive truth and respond by co-creating new realities. We will discuss how these four keys apply to parenting our children in Part 2 of this book. However, we can only offer what we possess, so please, take time to grow the skills mentioned so far. Joining a community of practice for encouragement and support might be helpful for you as you train. Sign up for an introductory call with LK10 to find out more about these groups.

If you are more of a "how to" person and eager to delve into the parenting side of the keys, then feel free to skip the next chapter and head straight to Part 2. However, if you want further illustration of these components lived out in real-life situations, the next chapter is for you. I will share a few stories of dismantling fear in various situations throughout my parenting career.

6
Fear Dismantling In Action

TRAINING MYSELF IN THE SKILLS NECESSARY to quickly wield these keys in real life situations has paid off many times over, allowing me to respond well to various kinds of parenting moments, everything from kids' emotional fits to their accidental injuries, to much worse. Here are a few examples of the components at work. These are entries from my personal journals that I have adapted here for readability—stories of difficult issues, some of which might be disturbing. However, they all end with finding an inner peace that surpasses all understanding.

JULY 2011 - SHE IS MINE

After spending the first ten years of her life in Uruguay, our daughter Allie was struggling emotionally. In this journal entry, I share when she began cutting herself to deal with emotional pain and how we used the keys to dismantle our fear so that we could help her build resilience.

Allie, 10 years old, has been up and down emotionally. We have amazing, playful moments followed by her melting down in anger and pushing us away. It is as if the intense joy we are now experiencing as a family allows her to feel some of her pain from past traumas. There appears to be a lot of pain there. Mourning the loss of her extended family because we lived in Uruguay. Grieving over the bullying she has experienced for years now in her Spanish-speaking schools. A lot has happened in her short little life. On Thursday, the climax hit. She had several fits of anger.

As I tucked her into bed, we reviewed the day, the appreciation moments as well as how big the harder feelings had been for her. As she talked of the harder feelings, she showed me her arm. Apparently, she had gotten so angry earlier in the day that she cut herself. We knew a few older children in our Uruguayan family and community who had begun cutting themselves. It seemed to be the going thing with teens that year.

My heart was broken. I did not know what to do or say. I quickly took a few deep breaths and looked for Jesus. I could see Him right next to me at the edge of Allie's bed. Seeing His compassionate, fearless eyes gave me peace. I silently asked Him to guide me and direct the conversation.

With that assurance and soothing, I gently, cautiously began the conversation with Allie, doing what I could to attune to her. "Wow, you really have been in a lot of emotional pain, haven't you?"

She nodded, looking deeply sad.

"And it seems like you just don't know what to do to make the pain go away. Is that right? Did that help you?"

My question was honest and nonjudgmental, pointing to the fresh cut on her arm. I genuinely wanted to know if it made her feel better. Gentle curiosity in moments like this seems to work better than reacting out of my fear and sadness. When I express shock, dismay or fear, it usually triggers shame in her, and then she shuts down.

"I just wanted the pain on the outside to match how much pain was on the inside," she shared articulately.

We continued talking for an hour or so about the nature of joy and pain. How our family had recently been working to build joy, that amazing feeling we have when we are all glad to be together no matter what. But that ironically, when we build joy, we also increase our capacity to feel the pain that has been hiding inside of us. So, the question becomes "What are we going to do with our pain?"

As she pondered, I added, "Do you want to continue cutting to make it somehow feel better? Or do you want to learn other ways to deal with it?"

I could see the struggle inside of her. I continued to look at Jesus and pray silently for her.

"I want to learn other ways to deal with it, Mommy." she decided.

My relieved heart exhaled. Then, she continued, "Please take the knife. It is behind the bookshelf."

I let out a deep breath of relief and gratitude. I grabbed the knife and we continued processing.

"The normal in our family, when you were young, was tense and somewhat conflicted," I began. "Your daddy and

I would sometimes get distracted by our own emotional worlds and you were sometimes lost in the middle, unseen and emotionally alone. But now, we know how to build joy in our family. And the norm is changing to a place of belonging, where we are more present, more relational, and so glad to see each other and be together. You are invited on this journey with us. Your baby brother and sister will know nothing different, but you will come to a place where you will have to decide whether you want to go where we are going. You can push us away and stay stuck in pain and tension and conflict. Or you can let us love you, let us enjoy you, let us see you, and begin to enjoy us as well. It takes practice and it will not be easy. The more joy that you let in, the more grieving will surface. However, the disconnected way we have lived has not been easy, has it?" I closed, looking down at her arm.

My beautiful Allie looked at me, and this time, decided to let love in. She asked about the exercises we do to help our brain grow relationally. We held each other and prayed. She rejected out loud any desire to ever cut herself again, and she asked God's protection to cover her.

After leaving her room I wanted to collapse in tears, the gravity of what had just happened weighing on me. All the worry and fear that I had been keeping at bay while talking with her came rushing forward like a stampede of heavy thoughts.

I went to my bedroom to seek comfort in God's presence. In my appreciation memories I could find Him quickly and sense His perspective.

Fear Dismantling in Action

"I have her, Toni. She is MINE." His words filled every nook and cranny in my mind, leaving no room for doubt, fear and worry. The words were accompanied by an image of Jesus on the cross, yet holding Allie in His strong arms. She was facing away from him and the powers of hell were fighting to rip her away. The image was so strong that it felt real. I watched as the scene unfolded.

He declared again, "SHE IS MINE!" causing a tidal wave of power to flow from His presence; all who wished Allie harm disappeared in the wake.

While I would have expected to be relieved with this image, there was still doubt. I expressed my doubt to Jesus, and the image continued to change. I saw Allie elbow Him in the side, drop to the ground as He let go, and take off running as fast as she could to get away from Him. I put my doubt into a question: "What if she pushes you away and runs?"

The image shifted again and Jesus launched Himself off of the cross. "I will go after her!" He affirmed, "Remember I am the good shepherd who goes after the lost sheep. I went after you, didn't I?"

Yes, He had gone after me. Memories flashed of Him meeting me in my own journey. He has always shown up for me when I needed Him. And while that brought comfort, I could not help but state the obvious. "That's comforting; however, she is more rebellious than I ever was."

Knowing my fears, He assured me, "I will go after her. She *is* mine!"

I finally began to weep out the fear, doubt and worry that had been lurking. As I focused on the image of Him chasing her down and not letting her go, all fear dissipated. Peace came and left me humbled…dare I say, expectant.

I bowed to Him, humbled and overwhelmed by His strength, His power, His love. I rose with an internal peace that no one could possibly understand.

2014 - UNDER PHYSICAL ASSAULT

The other day, I was on my way home from picking up my four- and five-year-old children from school when I got a call from my 13-year-old Allie, who was five minutes away from me at the house. "Mommy, I called the emergency doctor to the house because I am in pain. They think it is appendicitis. Would you like them to take me to the hospital in the ambulance, or would you like to take me?"

I could not believe this was happening. Matt, my husband, was out of town leading a short-term mission team. It would take too long to get him back. I wanted to take her but would need to find someone to care for the little ones. I was only five minutes away from the house, so I continued straight there.

As we turned into my neighborhood in Montevideo, Uruguay, apparently, I almost cut someone off in traffic as I made a left-hand turn approaching our street. I had not seen the car coming. I only realized it when he pulled up close to my bumper and honked at me to let me know he had been forced to slow down because of my turn. I felt horrible and waved at the man behind me, trying to tell him

I was sorry. My mind, of course, had been on Allie at home alone with a possible case of appendicitis.

The man then did something unimaginable. He sped up, swerved around me and pinned my car between his and the dumpster just a block from my house. I was confused and scared. Within seconds, the man was approaching my car with an infuriated look of malintent on his face. I could feel my heart rate rise. Fear was active, and rightly so. I had heard of road rage before but had never been a victim of an attack such as this.

In the few seconds before the man arrived at my car door, my skill practice took over. I instinctively began to center myself by breathing deeply, calming my body and mind. I heard my own voice calmly say, "Jesus help."

Remembering I had Matt and Annie in the car with me, I locked the doors and searched for my cell phone, thinking I would try to call the police.

The man approached my window screaming profanities at me in Spanish and began banging on my car window, demanding that I roll it down so that he could talk to me. He then tried to open the door. When he could not get to me, he continued insulting me over and over again.

I was calm even though I was afraid. I could sense God in the car with me. I continued breathing deeply and asked for God's presence to guide me in what to do.

I looked at the man eye to eye with only millimeters of glass between us. His eyes were filled with so much hate as he continued to angrily demand that I roll down the only thing protecting me from him.

I very respectfully replied in Spanish, "NO, I'm not going to roll down my window because you are being very disrespectful."

He got angrier, and I feared for my life. He continued to bang on the glass with such force that I quietly whispered under my breath, "God please keep it from breaking!"

I could feel God holding me together so the kids would not be alarmed. I glanced behind me to check on them as they both asked, "Why is that man so angry, mama?" They did not seem afraid at all, only curious.

It was so clear that my ability to quiet and connect with God at that moment was crucial to my being able to be fully present to their emotional needs. I managed to gently tell them that everything was going to be fine, that the man was very angry and that they needed to pray that God would intervene.

As I turned my attention back to the man, I breathed again and tried to sense God with me. "What do I do, Papa? How do I get us out of this? Please help!"

My mind cleared and I could understand some of the words the man was shouting about me.

"You are an idiot. You are an imbecile. You are a..." The list went on and on; some of the words I had never even heard.

In seconds, countering words formed in my mind: "Toni, even if you had cut this man off in traffic, you still do not deserve to be treated this way. You are Mine. You are My beloved child!"

Armed with this defense, I turned and looked my attacker right in the eyes, nose to nose, and said, "No," shaking my head back and forth, "I am not all those things you are saying. I am a beloved child of God."

As soon as the words left my lips, the man stopped instantly and backed away from the car with his hands up in the air as if I were holding him at gunpoint. He shook his head and ran away.

I could not believe it. I was thankful and relieved that the attack had ended.

I arrived home, put the kids to play for five minutes so I could ground out the pain and anger I had just absorbed into my soul. I remember going to my bedroom. I only had a few minutes before I had to take Allie to the hospital and deal with her possible appendectomy.

My body instinctively did the Shalom for my Body exercises, which released the shock of the event into tears of relief. Then, I sensed the thoughts: "Call your husband. You need to hear his voice. It will give you the strength necessary to turn your attention to getting Allie to the hospital."

I knew I would probably need to process more later, but after our 2-minute phone call, I had what I needed to be able to be present for my children in the next ordeal we were about to face. I got them to a friend's house and calmly headed to the hospital with Allie.

Eight hours later we discovered she was okay. No appendicitis, just a severely pulled muscle.

Once all the action and drama of the day subsided, I was so thankful to have had the skills I needed to get through these moments calmly and peacefully with my children.

2014 – Healing after Trauma

Here I am, Lord, coming for healing from what happened a few days ago with the angry man. In my imagination, we are there in our spot on the beach.

"What in the world happened to me on Monday?" I begin as You hold me close. "The kids were sick. I was a victim of road rage. I spent eight hours in the emergency room with Allie only to find out that it was a pulled muscle and *not* appendicitis. And there is a short-term mission team here whom we are supposed to be caring for! Where were You during the attack?"

"I was in the passenger seat right next to you, keeping you and the kids calm," as He begins, and as a smile comes across my face because I can see Him there. "I was inside of you keeping you calm for your kids. I was in the glass not breaking. And I was in your response, 'I am a child of God.'"

I can feel Him there in the memory inside of me, beside me, holding the window together. I am filled with gratitude and thankfulness. I am satisfied with how I responded, and I'm thankful that He gave me the right words to say to make the angry man leave.

Usually sensing Jesus with me in a traumatic memory is enough to bring complete healing to heart and mind. But for some reason, this offense is different. While

Fear Dismantling in Action

I see Jesus there, I also see the man's angry face. And the angry face is closer to me and bigger than Jesus's. It is as if the man's angry eyes are etched in my physical brain. I cannot shake his glare. No matter where I look, no matter who I am looking at, I only see his eyes. This triggers fear in me. I don't want to drive anymore. I feel vulnerable and exposed and unprotected. I find myself looking for the angry man in cars on the street. I'm afraid I will see him again. Will You help me, please?

"This is war, Toni. You live on the front lines where My Kingdom is expanding into the darkness. You have a great platoon around you. Rest in them. Their eyes will replace that man's eyes in time. Let your people look at you in the eyes and see how precious you are to them, especially the men in your community: your dad, Diego, Jackson, Matt, and of course, Me. The truth is that you are all vulnerable and weak. But know, My child, that you are *not* unprotected!"

My heart feels compassion for the man. I see him enslaved by his anger and probably deeply ashamed of the way he acted towards me. I wonder if he has ever yelled at his wife or his children the way he yelled at me. Do they know who he becomes when he is enraged? "Papa, I pray that You lead this man to you. I pray that he will learn how to still be himself even when he is angry. That he will learn to protect others from himself."

I am quieted. I am at peace. I will ask my friends in my community to look at me so that I can see their eyes enjoying me.

Asking the men in my family to look at me in the

eyes for a few minutes and let me see their love for me was a vulnerable thing to do. Their willingness to meet me that way made me feel so loved. After just two days of practicing these "joy smiles" with the four of them, I was completely restored. The angry eyes were gone and my fear of running into my attacker dissolved.

The crazy thing was that a few days later I actually did run into him in the airport parking lot. He was leaving as I was arriving. He was with two women. I had this impulse to walk up to him and tell him I forgave him, but in the end, I made eye contact with him and prayed for him. I do not know if he even recognized me, but if he did, I hope he saw love and forgiveness.

JANUARY 2015: HOW IT ENDS WITH ALLIE

Allie continued to struggle emotionally and relationally through all of junior high and we struggled to know how best to support her. As the bullying increased, she returned to cutting herself for relief. When the bullying and harassment turned sexual in nature, Allie shared with us that she felt suicidal. We decided to return to the USA for more professional support for our family.

"God, how does this end with Allie?" I asked one night, searching for a perspective that could carry me through whatever was to come. The image of Jesus chasing after her continued to play in my mind.

Instantly, she stops running, turns and faces Him, makes eye contact, almost playfully, and taps him on the chest as if playing tag. I realize she has stopped running because she has come to a 100-foot cliff.

Fear Dismantling in Action

Without hesitating, she turns and does a swan dive into the river below. I am breathless. Her courage, her beauty, her recklessness all collide.

As if on cue, Jesus dives after her just as gracefully. I see them below in the river swimming together, Jesus always just a little way behind. Then the image shifts and they both emerge onto a pebble bank where a packed lunch is awaiting them. Jesus prepares the picnic for her. She smiles. She looks happy. She is getting to know her Savior. She is letting Love in.

"This is how it ends," I hear God whisper in my ear. "I will have her! She is mine. She will let me love her. She will know joy and peace. Believe what you see."

I focused on the image and peace filled my entire body. No matter what happens, my Allie will end up with Jesus, letting him love and enjoy her. She will know her Maker.

Over the next three years of Allie's life, she would dabble in witchcraft, begin using drugs, and birth a baby girl only to see Baby Lily pass away minutes later. Through it all, I would grieve and seek God with my community about how to best respond. (I share some of these stories in the last chapter of this book.)

Matt and I would co-create new realities with God during these years. But none of them controlled the outcome of our daughter's pain or her choices. I learned to have peace no matter what Allie was feeling, choosing, experiencing or suffering. No matter what danger she would find herself in.

This image of how it ends is seared into my heart and mind. I am thoroughly convinced that she will one day let her Creator and Healer enjoy her, on this side of heaven or beyond. I know she is His. He knows her pain and He will never let her go. Nothing is beyond His repair. Nothing.

*****

Parenting out of joy and peace instead of fear is no small task. It will demand all the skills we possess. I only have these skills now because I have intentionally trained myself with incredibly helpful coaches and a community of practice. There are no parenting books that could have told me how to be the best parent that day under those situations. Showing up in those moments is not about what you know, it is about who you are and what automatic skills take over when you are under stress.

The skills of recognizing fear and realizing you are not alone are necessary to develop. Once you have made them habits by practicing them daily, receiving truth and co-creating new reality will flow into building a resilient family.

Part 2

Building a Resilient Family

7

Parenting As Children of God

THE SAYING, "We cannot give what we do not have," is 100% true in parenting. According to Dr. Allan Shore, by the time our children are three years old, we, as their principal caregivers, have completely reproduced our relational skills (or lack thereof) within their brains. This means that if we do not have a strong joy base, they will not have one either. If we do not have the ability to quiet our internal worlds, their internal worlds will remain chaotic.

This is why I spent the first half of this book on practicing and developing skills that put us in intimate relationship with ourselves and God, allowing Him to reparent us with all of the love, joy, peace, patience, kindness, goodness, gentleness and self-control that is the fruit of His Spirit. It begins with us recognizing our own need and being "reborn" into a new family, looking to God as our principal caregiver. Like a child with a parent, the more time we spend in interactive moments with God (Father, Son and Spirit) the more God transforms our minds and fills in many of the relational skill gaps that we have from our own families of origin.

As God becomes our parent, the people of God ideally become an extended family with whom we are able to see God more fully, practice skills and grow in relationship. Giving and receiving in a life-giving, intergenerational community affords us the opportunity to not only see the multi-faceted wisdom of God, but also fill in areas of maturity that are lacking. Unfortunately, many do not find this level of relational training or discipleship within the church. For hundreds of thousands of people, church means listening to a sermon and singing a few songs on a designated day of the week. While this type of gathering has its plce, it alone will neither retrain our brains nor build the skills we are missing. This can only happen in close relationships with those who have the emotional and spiritual maturity we are lacking. "Iron sharpens iron," as Proverbs tells us. We become like those we associate with.

Accumulating more intellectual truth and knowledge is not sufficient for character transformation. Sustainable growth can only take place through seeing, feeling, sensing and hearing God or others who love us. We have the ability to sense God in very tangible ways through our imagination, much as we see in the Bible when God gives images, visions and dreams. God redeems our imaginations for His use as we train ourselves to sense the Divine presence there. Then our relationship becomes experiential, not merely intellectual.

As stated earlier, it generally takes about three years to fully reproduce our own brain into our baby's mind. No wonder Jesus spent three solid years with His disciples. He was retraining their brains! His relationship with them made them so resilient that all of them would courageously submit themselves to incredibly difficult circumstances and even death.

To build resilient families, we need each other and we need an intimate relationship with our God who parents us, individually and communally. Out of these relationships, we gain all that we need to equip our children with the grit to face and overcome anything and everything.

The four components to building a resilient family are based on the same keys to overcoming our own fear. This makes it simple to remember and practice. Let's look at the four steps to dismantling fear and see how they are adapted in order to build resilient families. This involves:

1. Recognizing that feelings are active.
2. Reassuring your children they are not alone.
3. Recapturing and Redirecting their attention to truth.
4. Reaffirming their resilience through reflection.

8

Recognizing Feelings Are Active

RECOGNIZING FEAR IS PRESENT within our children involves family application of the three micro-skills:

1. Connecting relationally
2. Quieting our thoughts
3. Checking in with ourselves

When we approach building resilience in our children, there are two layers happening at all times. We need to be paying attention to our own fear levels and nesting into God's perspective *while* we train our children to do so as well. This involves simultaneously working these micro-skills within both ourselves and our children. This is definitely what I call "ninja-level" work!

A. CONNECTING RELATIONALLY

There are a few fun ways to help those around us turn on their relational circuit and access the relational side of their brains without their even knowing it. Asking our children if they are hungry or thirsty, hot or cold is oftentimes helpful, but sometimes not enough.

Recently, due to the COVID-19 shutdown, I have been online educating my 10- and 11-year-olds. Consequently, during the past year, I have had more practice in this area than in the last 20 years of parenting. Every day, my kids lose their relational capacity over and over again as they face challenges like not being allowed into a meeting, homework that is confusing or difficult, missed or late assignments, and the lack of joy strength they feel because they are isolated from their teachers and other children.

It has been a battle to stay relational myself with all the added stress. On many occasions, my children and I have cried, screamed, wanted to quit or throw the computer out the window. However, as we lean into practice, resilience is growing, slowly but surely.

My best "go to" for connecting all of us relationally has been, believe it or not, hot tea. No matter what is happening, when I ask if anyone wants a hot herbal tea or a chai, you can hear the exhale. Everyone takes a deep breath, calms down and declares, "YES!" This creates a pattern interrupt that stimulates sensations of warmth and friendship. It gives us time to cool off and reflect on what is happening. Tea has literally saved our day many times over.

I have also found that asking if they would like a hug can soften any moment and bring the relationship to the forefront.

In addition, my children know how to do the Shalom for my Body exercises (shared in detail in *The Joy Switch*).

Recognizing Feelings Are Active

When our youngest was 2 years old and our oldest was 12 years old, Matt and I regularly practiced these exercises with our children. One day, in conversation over dinner, our voices grew tense, possibly arguing about something. Much to our surprise, our discussion was interrupted by our 2-year-old's broken English. Tapping his chest as he exhaled, he advised us: "When I afraid, I trust you oh Lord."

We stopped dead in our tracks as we realized we were not being relational with each other. We both took some deep breaths and joined Matt in the exercise. The whole meal encounter had turned around for us. We were surprised at how our toddler could sense the tension and act to bring peace at such a young age. Out of the mouths of babes...

We can all help each other notice when we are coming across as non-relational if we can find a non-threatening, non-offensive way to do so. Chris Coursey recommends choosing code words for each member of the family. When someone recognizes you are engaging without your relational circuit on, they say their code word.

We loved that idea, but had a hard time remembering the words for each other, so ironically, when my son started tapping his chest that day, that became our "code." Tapping our chest and saying "when I am afraid" makes everyone laugh almost instantly. This way of reminding ourselves to be relational has even spread to our extended family.

More often than not, however, using the Shalom for my Body exercises to turn on our relational circuits when our relational capacity is low is the last thing any of us want to do. Especially if you are a 12- to 18-year-old! If the exercises are not already automatic habits, we forget about them completely. Which is why it is important to practice them regularly, so that when you need them the most, you remember what to do. It is also important to have several relationally-engaging practices on hand for any given moment.

Another brilliant way we have found to get ourselves relational as a family is holding our cat. Cats have an incredibly calming effect—at least ours does. In just a few seconds of holding Snow Paws, we feel calmer, closer to each other emotionally and less anxious. That is because in just a few seconds of holding her, oxytocin and serotonin are released into our bloodstreams. These hormones regulate anxiety, reduce depression, increase emotional bonding, stabilize our mood, and even help with sleeping, eating and digestion. I call this nature's cat scan.

However you get the family relational—with hot tea, hugs, breath awareness or holding a cat, there is then a clear pathway to sharing emotions, connecting heart-to-heart and building joy.

B. Quieting Our Thoughts

The most common way I have trained my family to quiet their thoughts is by taking deep breaths with them. When they were as young as 2 years old, they would come to me in tears trying to tell me what happened to them. I would look at them with empathy on my face, say "breathe!" and take a deep breath of my own. They would mirror my breath, and we would keep breathing and looking into each other's eyes until they could speak without tears interrupting. During that nonverbal moment, I was giving them a visceral experience that they were not alone in their emotion, as well as a physical practice they could use to calm themselves down and collect their thoughts and feelings.

We did that so many times that they have now learned how to calm their own emotions when necessary. Emotions can feel so big that they overtake us. Yet by being there for our children and helping them get relational and quiet, they learn how to feel their emotions but not get lost in them. This type of training continues throughout our entire lives. It is vital to relating well to each other and growing the inner strength necessary to face anything.

C. CHECKING-IN WITH OURSELVES

In our family we practice checking-in during meals together, two to three times a day. We each take turns (around two minutes each) sharing how we are feeling, and no one is allowed to correct or fix the person sharing. It is time for connecting.

Using the LK10 model, we say, "I'm checking-in as..." and we name all the emotions we are feeling. Then we explain each one. This practice has helped train my children to be aware of emotions and how they affect us.

When our children were very small, we helped them name their feelings. By looking into their faces, hearing their voice intonation and observing their actions, we would empathetically state what we saw.

"You look angry right now. Are you feeling angry?" (Asked with my eyebrows ruffled and lips pouted.)

"Wow! You are jumping up and down and smiling. It looks to me like you are excited. Is that what you're feeling?"

Helping our children name their emotions is a critical component in being able to understand emotions and to find joy in the midst of them.

Checking-in around the lunch or dinner table is how we *practice* emotional awareness. The goal is to acquire skills that are then used effectively in real-life situations throughout the day, so that in any given moment, our children can sense what they are feeling, why they are feeling it, and how that's affecting them physically, mentally and emotionally.

My extroverted 10-year-old son, Matt, actually walks around the house sharing his feelings regularly without being asked or prompted.

"I'm so happy today, Mom, because of the snow. It makes me feel energized and alive!"

"I am just so sad that Jay has moved. I think I need a hug."

"I miss my friends and going to school. Online educating is so hard!"

"I am disappointed that we cannot have lasagna tonight for dinner."

"Thank you for being my mom! You're the best mom ever. I love you."

Most of the time, he just needs a hug, an acknowledgement, something that lets him know he is "felt."

Even my introverted Anne, now 11-years-old, shares regularly without being asked, just more one-on-one.

"I am so happy to have a kitten. She brings me such warmth and peace."

She processes much of her feelings inside of her and needs less support moment by moment. She even seems to feel less strongly than the other children and is more stable and easier going.

And then there is Allie, the now 20-year-old who calls regularly to check in with the ups and downs of her week. It is either one extreme or the other with her, always deep, tender and dramatic. She spices up our lives and reminds us that life is worth feeling all that comes with it!

Our 30-year-old, Hilary, checks in three times a week in a more structured way. Our time is mutual as we both share intimately from our hearts about our lives, marriages, joys and struggles.

For me, practicing checking-in with my husband and children keeps my eye on the prize: heart-to-heart connection. Under pressure, it is easy for me to become a drill sergeant or taskmaster. However, watching for feelings keeps their hearts front and center. I am reminded to stay relational as I love them, receive from them and train them.

Once we know feelings are active, be it one of the primary negative six (anger, shame, fear, disgust, sadness, hopeless despair) or more positive emotions (peace, joy, love, happiness, hope) we can then be with our children in those emotions, reassure them they are not alone, and train them to find God there as well.

9

Reassuring Your Children They Are Not Alone

AS GOD PARENTS US, delights in us and assures us that the Spirit is closer than our breath, we have the ability to see how big our children's emotions are and help them find their way back to joy.

Just as joy is the foundation for a secure bond with God, it is also the foundation for a secure attachment with our children. They need to know that nothing they could ever possibly feel is powerful enough to separate them from our love. They need to know we are not afraid of their feelings and that we have what it takes to stay connected to them even when emotions get heated or cause a meltdown.

With our little ones, this attuning to their emotions happens a hundred times a day. They stumble, fall and look for us as they decide whether to cry or not. If we are there, we see the emotion in their eyes and name it.

"That was scary, wasn't it? You fell down and bumped your head."

The simple act of naming their feelings for them and explaining what happened while looking into their eyes and mirroring their concern on our faces assures them that they are not alone. They are ready to hear the truth.

"It's okay. You're not hurt. Up you go."

And off they go, running and playing again as if nothing ever happened. Except that something profoundly important did happen. We attuned to them.

Attunement, according to renowned child psychiatrist, Dr. Dan Siegel, is all about feeling *seen* and *felt*. Attuning with your child means perceiving their emotions, making sense of what is going on in their minds, and responding in a connecting, timely way.

It involves sensing "their internal mental state in a way that lets them know that we get them, so they can 'feel felt' and understood on a profound and meaningful level." It is about focusing less on a child's specific behavior or external observable events of a situation, and more on what's happening inside (*The Power of Showing Up*, p.110).

Attunement builds trust and is the process by which we form relationships.

I could have said to the fallen toddler: "Nothing happened; you are fine; don't cry."

However, that would invalidate their internal experience, which is the opposite of seeing them. Something *did* happen even if that something seemed insignificant to me. By naming it for them ("That was scary, wasn't it?") and making sense of it ("You fell down and bumped your head") they feel felt and seen and are ready for encouragement: "It's okay. You will be alright. Up you go."

As my children get older, this process becomes a little more challenging. Many times, when they feel strong emotions, it is not always clear what is happening or what they are feeling. So, I have to check my relational circuit, take a deep breath and draw on Divine collaboration by asking God to guide me and help me know how best to interact.

Just the other day, I was sitting with my 10-year-old son, Matt, helping him with his schoolwork. He seemed agitated and short-tempered. I quickly became frustrated. I felt my impatience rise as my speech became more measured and punctuated. He could sense my frustration, and I could tell it was amplifying his distress.

As he began to cry, I paused, and started using the keys. I took a deep breath, recognized my emotions, sensed God's presence in the room with me and silently asked God for help. I sensed the phrase, "Be curious." And with that bit of truth, I could now co-create a new reality with God.

I began by making a curious observation:

"Honey, you seem very upset and short-tempered. That is not who you normally are. Is there something else going on that could be bothering you?"

He paused, calmed down a bit, and began to think. "Yes, I think I am hungry. But I also miss Jay."

It all made sense now. This was not about homework at all. He was missing his best friend who had moved to

Korea three months prior. My son was in attachment pain, the pain we feel when a loved one is not present for us and everything in the world seems harder, darker and more frustrating. My heart became tender and soft. I asked if he wanted a hug, and he melted into my embrace and cried out his grief. It lasted for about two minutes, then he was back at homework with a newfound energy and strength. A yogurt was helpful as well.

This approach does not always work that quickly or effectively. However, the more we let Jesus emotionally attune to us, the more we will know how to attune to our own children. While doing so is not easy, it is the only way our children will be willing to hear the truth they so desperately need. Just like us, once they feel felt and seen, most of their emotional distress dissipates and they are willing to hear whatever truth they need to in order to grow and mature.

10

Recapturing and Redirecting Attention to Truth

The Role of Listening, Appreciation and Storytelling

FEAR IS SUCH AN ATTENTION GRABBER. Many of us scan our environment constantly to see what possible dangers could be ready to harm us. While there is a healthy amount of concern necessary in order to survive, too much focus on threats leaves us anxious and on edge.

Interestingly, psychologists say that our children's generation is the most anxiety ridden generation of all due to several factors, one being the social media phenomenon. Now, with COVID-19 isolating more and more children and teens, anxiety and depression are at all-time highs.

Making time to check in with our children and attune to them definitely creates a sense of belonging and feeling cared for that is essential in the mental health of our children. But how do we train their brains (and our own) to automatically turn to our Source of truth for belonging, understanding, comfort and correction? We cannot force them to receive Truth, but we can recapture their imagination by building habits within them—physical, mental, emotional and spiritual habits—that redirect them to receive from the Life-giver.

Recapturing and redirecting our and our children's attention to "whatever is true, whatever is noble, whatever is right, whatever is pure, whatever is lovely, whatever is admirable," as Philippians 4 encourages, is no small task. There are so many other competitors for our attention, short-term fixes that bring pseudo-joy. Video gaming, social media and unlimited TV shows, for example, did not even exist before the '80s. While there was Atari, it was hardly the attention grabber that the gaming world is today.

Reclaiming our attention involves training and practice. As I have noted, that often looks different from just living life. The training must be intentional in the beginning, even as it feels uncomfortable or unnatural. It is unnatural…until you learn the skill. Then it becomes natural!

No exception to the rule, my children don't exactly love the training part of it, but I have seen them benefit greatly from it when they are in distress and need to connect to a source of love and truth beyond themselves.

Because appreciation is the quickest way I know to help myself and others connect with the Way, the Truth and the Life, I always try that route with my children…if they are willing. I know my words of encouragement are necessary, but sometimes our words as parents just fall to the ground. However, connecting them to the Divine Holy

Recapturing and Redirecting Attention to Truth

Spirit within them resources them and teaches them to seek Truth for themselves and find it as often as possible.

THE PRACTICES: LISTENING AND APPRECIATION

As close to daily as possible, usually at dinner or bedtime, our family practices taking a minute or two in silence to pay attention to how God feels about being with us and what He might want us to know. I encourage the children to write down the first thoughts or impressions that come to mind, knowing we can discern later whether what we sensed is from God or just ourselves.

It is a simple practice that literally takes a few minutes, yet we have to move heaven and earth to make it happen! The kids LOVE checking in, but listening involves quieting...and that is where the training (read: intentional) comes in.

When they were little, this was fun because little ones are so playful. Once, for example, one of the children said, "I see our dog in my mind. Is that from God?"

"It could be," I replied. "Ask God what He might want you to know about the dog."

Laughing and smiling, she said, "The dog is licking me and loving on me! I think God is telling me that He loves me as much as the dog loves me! I feel tickly all over!"

God communicates constantly. In John 1, Jesus is referred to as the Word of God who existed long before the Bible as we know it was formalized into a Book. In John

16:13, the Holy Spirit is called the Spirit of Truth who comes to "guide you into all the truth."

If God is communicating since the beginning of time, wanting to guide us into all truth, why would we not remove everything that hinders us from hearing and sensing what the Source of all life is saying? Recapturing the attention of our children by training them to sense God's presence is a skill that will ultimately give them the resilience they need to face anything. Inner joy and peace are the foundations to resilience, and they come through a very real relationship with the Divine, not a relationship with cognitive truth or a book.

Now, to be clear, we value the Bible. My younger children continually devour their comic book Bibles. We also read scripture regularly together as a family. However, when we read, we try to recapture our imaginations and engage with our whole selves. We pay attention to what stands out to us and what stirs in our hearts. Then we ask God what stirs in His heart as we read the story of His relationship to His people. We read with Immanuel, *God with us*. Which, of course, takes us back to the fundamental practice of connecting to this Divine presence.

The daily two-minute practice of listening with our children, learning to discern God in our imaginations, souls and inner worlds, forms a habit that will automatically redirect them to the Living God for their comfort, direction, truth and life.

Some days we do not sense any new insight from God, just a steady source of "I am so glad to be with you!" We learn that just being together with God and feeling loved is enough and possibly the most important part of this relationship.

As a parent who is driven to see my children develop well, it is easy to get wrapped up in performance issues. My thoughts turn to, "Are my children hearing from God or not? Are they really 'getting it'? Am I a failure if they do not sense anything?" When these thoughts come, I am reminded by God that it is the *practice* that is important, not their immediate success in hearing.

When I was 19 years old, I was a counselor in training with the youth group at our church. Don Gilbert was our fearless leader, and I was so excited about the first Youth Volunteer leader retreat. It consisted of three days set aside to train and equip us for all we would face as pastors of youth. During that time, we sat in silence four times a day, praying for "our kids" (as we called the junior and high school students). We logged probably four hours of silence, listening and praying per day.

When I returned home, I was shocked to find that my body actually longed for silence, listening and prayer! It was a physical craving, a habit created in just three short days. This is the type of physical habit I am talking about forming with ourselves and our children.

This daily practice of silence, listening, and two-way prayer is essential if we want to create a neurological automatic response to seek God's perspective on everything in life, especially how we feel and what we need to know.

The practice of silence alone has enormous benefits mentally, emotionally and physically, even if the children never sense God. Research shows that some of these benefits include stress reduction, decreased anxiety, decreased depression, reduction in pain, improved memory, reduced blood pressure, reduced heart rate, decreased metabolism, increased melatonin, and increased efficiency in the brain's capacity for attention[6].

As if these benefits alone were not enough to encourage us to sit in silence with our children a few minutes every day, thankfully, we get all of these benefits plus the Truth, the Way and the Life constantly communicating love and guidance our way, longing to be with us.

Because it is practice, it can feel mundane. But it sets the stage for some beautiful God interventions during real life situations. (I share more of these in Chapter 6 – Fear Dismantling In Action.)

APPRECIATION PRACTICE

Finding and sharing appreciation memories is also key in helping to recapture and redirect our attention. The benefits of feeling appreciation are as many as they are for sitting in silence.

As close to daily as possible, my family tells appreciation stories. I will sometimes begin with a memory of appreciating my children or my husband. "Memories of us" build belonging, community and secure relational bonds between us. Plus, sharing moments when we have

---

[6] See Dr. Daniel J. Siegel's book *Aware: The Science and Practice of Presence*

appreciated being with each other just feels good! Watching the recipient's face light up as I tell them how it made me feel to be with them sends jolts of joy back my way. For example:

"Anne, my favorite part of the day today was when you came into my room this morning and just sat on my bed and talked with me for an hour. I felt close to you and amazed at how much you are growing. I enjoyed you so much; it was like a mini vacation where time stopped and all that mattered was us together. Thank you!"

To prompt the sharing, I might ask one of us: "What was your favorite memory from today? And how did it make you feel?"

Whether at lunchtime, dinnertime, bedtime, or any other moment we are together, the children have come to expect this question, and they hate not having an answer. They now look for and collect their beautiful moments of joy and connection throughout their day instead of only retaining the difficult moments.

As we share our memories, we make sure to include the physical side of the memory as well as the emotions. Things like:

- Where was I?
- What did I hear?
- What did I see?
- What did I feel physically?
- How did that make me feel emotionally?

Each person imagines the memory and relives the whole experience as they tell the story. This allows the sensations to be felt again throughout the person's body, and it helps others enter into the experience as well.

I also write down some of the children's stories to keep on hand for when they are in distress and need them. It is hard for a person in distress to remember a moment of appreciation. That is why we practice telling and collecting these stories: To have an arsenal ready when heavy feelings or difficult situations come.

Just last week, my highly introverted daughter, Anne, was faced with a difficult school assignment. She had to memorize and perform a monologue. I knew she was capable of doing it with no problem, but she was determined that it was too hard and that she did not want to do it.

Now, when Anne decides she does not want to do something, feelings get very big for her and she becomes overwhelmed with anger and hopeless despair. Anne is normally such an easy-going, stable person that this type of meltdown rarely happens. However, when it does, I can easily get overwhelmed as well, making things much worse.

On this particular day, I offered to help Anne. After all, I had been in several plays during my adolescent years and remembered quite a few memorization techniques. She immediately declined, making excuses for why this was going to be impossible.

I stepped back from the situation. Realizing fear was rising in me, I began breathing deeper and making sure I

Recapturing and Redirecting Attention to Truth

was relational. In my imagination, I quickly found my quiet, internal space with the God of the Universe. I was transported to the beach where Jesus and I talk frequently. I needed to know I was not alone. I needed Truth to hold me and guide me through this. It is very challenging to get Anne unstuck and move her forward in moments like this. I did not want to make things worse, and I did not want to hurt her. In my imagination, on the beach with Immanuel, I began praying for her.

"God, please intervene with her. Help her come to a place where she would like help. Help turn this. What do you want me to do?"

I was kneeling before Him, as I often do, ready for His orders.

"Wait," I heard him say.

Okay. With my fear gone, I took another breath, left Anne in His hands and returned to making dinner.

After some time, she came to me again in complete emotional distress. She was crying and saying she didn't want to do this and could not do this.

Compassion welled within me. I named what I saw and attuned to her.

"This feels really big for you, doesn't it? You really don't want to do this, do you?"

She shook her head up and down and then side to side.

"Can I help you?" I asked again, feeling Jesus guiding me.

Through her tears, she said, "Yes."

I placed my hand on her hand and began.

"I can see this is distressing for you and feels very, very difficult. It looks like the most difficult part of this is facing your own will. You clearly do not want to do this. I don't think the problem is that you cannot do it. I think the problem is you just don't want to."

She nodded in affirmation.

"Would you be willing to go to an appreciation memory?" I asked.

She nodded through her tears but contested: "I don't know how that'll help!"

Often, when we are struggling, it's hard to see how this process works. So, I moved forward gently with a memory she had shared with me just yesterday.

"Remember going on the zipline yesterday with your friends?"

She nodded.

"You told me how you could feel the breeze on your face, as you flew through the air in the harness. Can you see yourself there in your imagination?"

She nodded and tears began to subside.

"Great!" I said. "Now, ask Jesus where He was in that moment and tell me what you see in the image.

"He was at the end of the zipline ready to receive me into His arms."

"Wow!" I said, actually surprised and relieved that she saw Him so quickly. I looked at Jesus in my imagination on the beach with deep gratitude for showing up for her.

"What happens when you land?"

"He holds me," she said.

"So, you are in His arms right now?"

She nodded.

"Tell Him how you feel about this project and ask Him what he thinks about it."

She cried and cried about how hard this task was. Once the wave of emotion subsided, she said somewhat sheepishly, "He says I need chocolate cake."

I giggled with her and quickly asked Jesus in my own imagination what He thought of that. The thought came to me that she was most likely experiencing some hormonal fluctuations due to her cycle. Further, I have read that chocolate can help balance those chemicals in the brain and body.

I shared this with Anne and said that maybe Jesus was helping her pay closer attention to her body and its needs. I told her I actually had some chocolate on hand for just these moments! She, of course, was surprised and elated.

Over a small piece of chocolate, I continued, "What else does Jesus say? Does He think this assignment is too much for you to handle?"

"No," she replied. Her face went soft. "He says I have what it takes."

I almost started crying myself as I saw the change come over her. Jesus had held her while she cried. He "felt" her, He was with her. And now, He was giving her what she needed to move forward. She had emotionally returned to herself.

"I just don't know how," she continued.

"How to do what?" I asked. "How to trust Him, or how to do the project?"

"How to memorize the script," she clarified, and then added the words that are the absolute most difficult for her personality to ask. "Can you help me?"

I was thrilled. We formed a plan together, jumped into the work, and she was 100% happily given over to the project. I could not believe my eyes. In 45 minutes, the crisis was over and we had recorded a fully memorized two-minute monologue!

Reclaiming and redirecting our children's attention to the Person who is truth is the most important task we can ever attempt as parents. Silent times of learning to listen coupled with telling appreciation stories and looking for Immanuel, these are the practices that turn impossible moments into our deepest victories.

Yet, these triumphs can go forgotten over time, and the lessons that we could learn fall unincorporated in our life unless we have the habit of reflecting on what we are experiencing. Reflection is the way to reaffirm their resilience, calling forth their identity and responsibility.

11

Reaffirming Their Resilience

The Role of Reflection in Calling Forth Identity and Responsibility

JOHN DEWEY, ONE OF THE MOST prominent philosophers, psychologists and educational reformers of the early 1900s, stated in his book, *How We Think*: "We do not learn from experience. We learn from reflecting on experience" (p. 78).

I have applied this principle in my academic and professional endeavors and even my personal growth. However, it did not occur to me until recently that this could help our children learn and grow. We could have incredible experiences like the one with my daughter Anne in the previous chapter, yet, without reflecting with Anne about what happened, how she came out of the crises and what she learned, that experience would be lost on her (and me), and neither of us would remember how to face the world differently in the future.

Reaffirming our children's resilience requires us to reflect with them on everything they experience, taking full advantage of their teachable moment. And, by way of reflection, we get to call forth their identity and their responsibility.

In my experience, reflecting with my children is just as hard as trying to sit in silence with them. No one likes to be still for long. I hold Hebrews 12:11 in my mind for encouragement. The Message puts it this way:

> *At the time, discipline isn't much fun. It always feels like it's going against the grain. Later, of course, it pays off handsomely, for it's the well-trained who find themselves mature in their relationship with God.*

While building resilience in our families involves building joy and belonging, playing together and having fun, it also includes training. Without training, our children will not mature emotionally, physically or spiritually. We humans are slow to learn and difficult to train. It takes daily effort over an extended time for practices to become habits that are then naturally incorporated into who we are.

Reflecting on our successes, our difficult moments, our emotional ups and downs and even our training is how we reaffirm our resilience, calling forth our identity and understanding our responsibility. While it is not necessarily fun for us or our children, it is essential if we want to grow and mature.

When I debrief with my children, I often draw from the same questions I use in my professional world of training adult educators and facilitators. I learned these questions years ago when I began training adult mentors in

Reaffirming their Resilience

Godly Play. Godly Play is an approach to children's Christian Education that helps them explore their faith through story, wonder and play. I have found these debriefing questions to be incredibly effective in all situations in life.

These are some of the reflection questions I use:

- What just happened? Form the story together.
- What was your favorite part?
- What part seemed most important?
- What did you do to help you get back to joy?
- How did you find Jesus?
- What questions did you ask Him?
- What is it like us to do when we feel overwhelmed?
- What will you do next time you feel overwhelmed? Or What will you do differently next time?
- Do you feel like you know how to find Jesus by yourself if you need to?

Below, I share the questions in the context of debriefing Anne around her monologue project.

First, we reviewed the story of what happened. Just doing that was incredibly valuable. As we pieced together the scenario that had unfolded the previous day, I could see what each of us remembered and what we had already forgotten. Comically, I had almost completely forgotten about the chocolate, while Anne had almost only remembered the chocolate!

After re-creating the story together, I began debriefing.

"What was your favorite part?" I asked.

"Definitely eating the chocolate cookie," Anne quickly replied. "As soon as it hit my taste buds, I felt better!"

I laughed with her and pressed in a bit more, "What part was most important for you?"

"I don't know," she replied, clearly uninterested. You have to remember she is 12! When we do any type of debrief that requires thought, she pushes back a little.

Knowing how hard this is for her, I begin calling forth her identity,

"You know, you really are incredibly smart, and it is like us in the Daniels family to think through things even when it's hard or when we would rather go read a book."

She playfully rolled her eyes and gave it a shot, "Maybe seeing Jesus on the landing. Being held by Him. And eating chocolate."

I nodded and laughed with her; I could tell we were not going to get too far from the chocolate.

"What did we do that helped you return to yourself?" I continued.

"Ate chocolate," she continued her *I-don't-wanna-think* attitude.

"But, how did you get to the chocolate? Do you remember?" I playfully added.

"By asking Jesus what I needed," she said.

I wanted to draw her back to the first steps that got her relational.

"And what led you to ask Him what you needed?"

"You shared an appreciation story with me, Mommy. That is what helped me return to myself."

I nodded, smiling and added, "And I shared the appreciation story because you asked for help. I know it is not easy for you to ask for help."

She nodded, then tiring of reflecting, begged: "Can I go now?"

"Almost. There are just a few more questions." I smiled and looked into her eyes.

"What would you do differently next time?"

"Next time, eat chocolate sooner," she said half joking. "I would ask for help sooner. I was just so mad that I had to do the assignment. My anger keeps me from moving forward. But I wasted so much time and energy just not wanting to do it."

I nodded, affirming what she was saying. Then I asked the last questions: "What do you take away from this whole experience? What do we tend to do in moments like this?"

Seeing that she was done thinking for the moment, I asked if I can sum it up. She nodded.

"It is like "us" to recognize we need help, realize we are not alone, and receive truth. You were lost in fear and anger and you could not get out. You could not see a way forward with this assignment because you could not get out of your anger and fear. Asking for help was a great idea.

Mommy shared an appreciation story that helped turn your relational circuit on. You immediately sensed Jesus there with you and He helped you connect with your body to see what you needed and to receive the truth that you could do this assignment."

I could see that she was following me, although I knew it would take much practicing before she realized how to get unstuck by herself.

"Good job," I encouraged her. "I love you!"

"I love you too," she hugged me, and off she went.

Reflecting on the past in this way helps us write the future. The question, "What is it like the Daniels to do in this situation?" is an identity question. It helps us remember who we are no matter what emotion is trying to overtake our response. With proper training, we can learn to remain who we are and act like ourselves no matter what is happening around us.

MATT DRONES ON AND ON

One more example of the keys in action is the day Matt got his drone stuck in a tree…twice! We were getting ready to leave for school when Matt came running in for the second time with tears streaming down his face.

"I got my drone stuck in the tree again."

Quite frustrated, my sigh said it all. I took a deep breath, realizing he felt terrible enough already, and quietly got the extension pole to try to maneuver the drone free.

After climbing onto a dangerous ledge, I struggled and struggled. As my frustration grew, I could hear Matt below absorbing my negative energy into himself.

"Matt, why don't you go inside while I finish up here. Mommy is not frustrated with you. I am just upset that I cannot get the drone down. I will be in soon."

When the drone was finally set free (in Jesus' name!), I entered the house to find Matt still crying. I could tell he was in a complete emotional overwhelm. Still frustrated myself, I paused and did my Rs as fast as I could.

"God, how do I engage with Matt in a way that is redemptive, restorative, and helpful instead of harmful?"

Relational and sensing Jesus with me, I moved in to co-create a new reality.

"Hey Matt...can you tell me how you are feeling?"

Through tears, he managed: "I feel like I am a bad person because I got the drone stuck twice in the tree. What kind of idiot does that?"

I sensed Jesus holding me back from responding. Instead, He prompted me to create a moment where Matt could hear directly from Him.

"Let's work the Rs with Matt. He's old enough to learn. Train him!"

I smiled at the opportunity and carefully moved forward.

"Matt, I am wondering how you felt right before the drone got stuck in the second tree?"

His face lit up and tears stopped, "Aww Mom! It was so high! It was amazing! I was so excited!"

Recognizing this was an appreciation moment, I invited him to describe the whole scenario.

"Close your eyes and tell me in detail everything you remember. Where exactly were you standing? What direction were you facing? How high was the drone exactly?"

After he enthusiastically painted the entire picture, I continued, "Look around and ask Jesus where He was? Do you see Him there in your memory in your imagination?"

"Yes, Momma, He is right next to me. He is so happy to be flying the drone with me! He is saying, 'Fly it higher. Fly it higher. You can do it. Go for it!'"

By this time, we were laughing together. It was just like Jesus to call us to risk a little and go beyond what we are capable of.

"Then what happened," I asked.

"Then, I flew it higher and it got turned around and I tried to control it, but it was too difficult and it went right into the tree."

"Okay. Stay in your memory and look at Jesus now. He is right there next to you. Tell Him how you are feeling and ask Him how He feels about you and about the drone getting stuck in the tree."

Matt looked at Jesus in his imagination. I could tell he was doing the work. Then he smiled and said: "He is glad to be with me. He is glad I took the risk. He says that I am not bad because I got it stuck again. That what I was doing was really hard and that even a pro-drone flyer might have made that same mistake. It is not because I am bad or stupid. He said it takes practice and it is okay to fail."

"Wow! Matt, how does that make you feel?"

"I am happy and ready to go to school!"

After that, we got in the car and I wanted to work the last R: Reaffirm their resilience through reflection. So, I asked Matt to tell me the overall story of what had happened.

"I got my drone stuck twice. I was overwhelmed. I felt bad inside. You got it out for me and then we found Jesus and He made me feel better. He told me I was not stupid at all and that there is room to fail and learn from our mistakes."

"Great!" I continued debriefing him. "Where did you find Jesus first?"

"In the good part of the memory where I was happy. Like you teach us, Mommy, in the appreciation!"

"And then what did we ask Jesus?"

"I asked Him how he felt about me and what He wanted me to know about losing the drone again."

"Yes! And How did you feel after Jesus spoke truth to you?"

"Wonderful, happy, encouraged."

"Well done, Matt. Now…" I continued as we pulled up to drop him off at his Middle School, "If you are at school or at a friend's house and Mommy is not there, and you need to get back to joy from strong feelings, it sounds like you know how to do that. Do you feel like you do?"

"Yes!" he exclaimed proudly. "Yes, I do!"

I smiled. "It is like us, when we are overwhelmed, to find Jesus and let Him help us get back to joy. This is our identity and our responsibility."

Indeed, it is.

THE POWER OF DO-OVER STORIES

What if I had not handled the situation well? That is the beauty of reflection. When I realize things did not go as well as I had hoped, I can imagine myself responding in a different way in that situation. Realizing how I would have liked to have handled a moment, and then expressing it in story format, tells my brain how to handle similar situations in the future. It also has the power to repair a relationship when I have damaged it by responding out of fear, anger or one of the other darker emotions. And If I do not know how I could have responded differently, reflecting with someone else gives me feedback and ideas for how I could have acted more like myself.

For Anne, her "do-over" was to ask for help sooner and realize her hormones might be affecting her strong feelings.

"Do-overs" can be quick and easy, but so powerful for repairing a relationship. The other day, I was so scared that my son was missing a Zoom meeting that I ran through the door practically yelling, "OH NO!"

Both of my children jumped to the ceiling in fear at the sound of my hysteria.

Matt, however, was actually in his meeting. Unfortunately, he now had a surge of adrenaline pumping through his body from the sound of my panic.

After his meeting was over, I went to him and told my redo.

"Matt, I am so sorry I ran through the door screaming in fear. I bet that really scared you. Next time, if I am afraid like that, I will come in quietly and check to see if you are in a meeting."

He was incredibly relieved. The redo had the power to almost rewrite for him what happened minutes before. It was almost as good as doing right in the first place. Almost…

The benefits to making mistakes is that we get to model for our children that we all mess up, and that there is a way to make things right and learn from our shortcomings.

To become a resilient family, we all must experience these types of emotional bumps many times a day and then reflect on how we handled them—what was helpful, what was not, and what we will do differently next time. Reflecting in this way draws out our identity and responsibility to handle ourselves well.

Recognizing our strong emotions, realizing we are not alone in them, and receiving Truth allows us to respond with creativity and strength. No matter what circumstance we find ourselves in, we know we have what it takes to overcome because we have practiced dismantling our fear and letting the mysterious cooperation with the Divine co-create new realities—those we never dreamed possible.

12

Resilience Building In Action

Resilience is the ability to recover quickly from difficulties, or as some say, the ability to bounce back when life knocks you down. Here are a few more stories of life knocking us down, so to speak, and how we have bounced back.

Notice that co-creating new realities with God and bouncing back does not always mean it ends the way we want or expect. It means that God seems to reframe what is actually happening so that I can have peace through it, no matter what. It means I know how to grieve and feel the depth of sadness that the struggles of life here on earth entail. It means that we fear nothing because we have a different perspective than the one being lived out in front of us.

Our stories are not wrapped up tightly with a pretty bow on them. We are all in process and messy at times. Sometimes, we bounce back but have lost some air or our shape. Maybe, we even limp with grief for a while. Like Gandolf said at the end of *Return of the King*,

> *Well, here at last, dear friends, on the shores of the Sea comes the end of our fellowship in Middle-earth. Go in peace! I will not say: do not weep; for not all tears are an evil.*

My husband likes to say our tears are liquid prayer. Let's just say that through the most difficult parenting years of my life, I prayed liquid prayers…a lot! These tears keep us resilient, for they allow us to grieve what is lost so that we can co-create what is to be.

APRIL 2015

Returning to the States after 18 years abroad was no walk in the park for any of us. Allie continued to spiral downward. She began smoking, practicing witchcraft and exploring her sexuality. Here are some snippets of the level of brokenness and fear I felt and how I found peace and guidance consistently in the arms and perspective of the Divine:

"I'm so worried about Allie, Papa God," I come desperately pacing back and forth in my imagination.

"Is that going to help you?" Jesus asks.

Stopping me from pacing, He looks deeply and compassionately into my eyes.

"What are you afraid of?"

"That she will shut us out and turn her back on you."

There, I said it. I am so afraid of losing her.

Jesus continues His gentle inquiry, "Why do you fear that?"

This seems obvious, given that I just found out that Allie is practicing witchcraft and smoking. But I humor Him.

"Because of the pain it will bring to us all, and because I fear she will stop growing and stay in addiction."

"What if she does? You do realize that you cannot live her life for her, right? You've lived your life. And you've gotten to choose your own path. Only she can choose her path. You will help her make better choices, but you cannot do that while you are in fear. And by the way, you're doing a fine job as a mother."

I cry as He tries to encourage me. Feeling like a total failure of a mom, I push away His complement, letting it fall to the ground.

My daughter seems like the one with all the problems, and yet, Jesus is here revealing the lie that binds *my* heart. I believe that if I were a good parent, all this would be easier.

Jesus responds so unexpectedly: "Yes, I know that feeling. I was there once. Remember when I cried out 'Jerusalem, Jerusalem…how I have longed to gather your children together…and you were not willing.'[7] And these children of mine were killing prophets and stoning those I sent them! I know the grieving, as well as the cost."

---

[7] Matthew 23:37

Inspired, I beg, "Make me who I need to be to love her as she needs me to. She is worth my life. Help me give it for her."

"Trust me more with her," Jesus responds, as he pries her out of my clenched fists. "Trust that I'm working even when you don't know or see."

*****

Just a few weeks later I sensed fear active again. I was afraid I was not doing enough as a mom. Not giving my kids enough attention, time, instruction, love, etc. Not wanting to parent from fear, I sought God again.

"I'm here, my child," I sensed Jesus say.

"It's so dark inside my world that I can't see you," my confession was raw.

"Then sense me," He directed.

I could sense Him physically close, but it didn't make the pain go away. I tried going to an appreciation memory, but enjoying appreciation only seemed to make it worse. The sadness was too much to bear and the appreciation only released more sadness.

"What do I do?"

"Enjoy your children today. Stop trying to do more and just see them and enjoy them. They are amazing creatures!"

How could I enjoy my children when one of them was so lost? I expressed to him my anger, sadness and hopeless despair, not just over my daughter, but over the loss of the life I had to leave behind in Uruguay.

Anger flooded my body.

"We have given our life to You and to missions, yet our daughter is in so much pain. Why didn't you protect her?" I screamed. "She hates you! I barely know who she's become, and I fear for her mental health. If someone had told me that I would sacrifice my daughter for Uruguay, would I have gone?"

I fall into a heap at Jesus' feet.

"Not for a moment did I forsake you."

He whispers the words of my favorite song into my ear. And at the sound of the words, memories come of Jesus affirming His presence in my life every single step of the way, from birth all the way through to our calling to Uruguay, and our return to the States. He has been here. He has not forsaken us.

Jesus begins His truth-telling like only He can do.

"You are who you are because of the struggles you have had with your daughter. Remember when I told you it was no accident that I gave her to *you*. You needed her in order for your self-reliance to be broken. And she needed you as her mother because you are tenacious, and you do not give up. I am in your story from beginning to end. See it all."

Another memory surfaces. I see myself pregnant with Allie, rubbing my tummy. I was so happy to have her with me. I enjoyed her so much. I still enjoy her so much.

Anger subsides as I relinquish control. Overcome with how much I love my daughter, I focus on enjoying her, and the other children today. This is one small parenting assignment from Jesus that now, I think I can do.

MAY 2015 – ENNEAGRAM 4

A month later, we check our precious Allie into a Crisis Center.

We put some guardrails up for Allie tonight, lovingly and calmly. She did a good job listening and not lashing out, but when she realized we were taking her phone, she hit a complete emotional overwhelm and felt like she would hurt herself or us. She asked us to call the Crisis Center. We took her in and they wanted to admit her to a teen psych center for 3 to 5 days.

I ask the best Parent in the universe for advice.

"Papa, please be with her, fight for her, go after her and help her get answers for herself. I am holding her with you on the bank of the river. I see you loving her. I feel complete peace. Whatever it takes to get her there, I am willing to endure. Anything I need to know?"

"Yes," He responds. "I want you to study her Enneagram Type[8]. There are things about Allie's personality that you do not understand. Study her, seek to understand her, and see the immense beauty I have placed within her. You will help call it forth."

---

[8] For an introduction to the Enneagram System see: https://www.enneagraminstitute.com/how-the-enneagram-system-works

While Allie is in the hospital, I study. It turns out she is a 4 on the Enneagram, which explains a lot!

- She is capable of a depth of feeling that most people have no access to.
- She feels most alive when she is in raw emotion. She will feel at extremes, either super happy or super sad.
- She is fun-loving but also sensitive, and highly empathic. Which means that without knowing it, she feels deeply within her all the pain of the world gone wrong.
- If she can hold in balance the beauty and the pain, amazing creativity will be unleashed through her.

After reading the life tasks that this personality type needs, I feel resourced and relieved. All of her life I saw these extremes in her and the deep pain, yet I never knew this is part and parcel for many artists and prophets. Tears come as I realize how my daughter's heart has been under attack almost from day one. She is a beautiful, powerful young woman, flooded by pain.

"Papa, set her free. Give her all the joy and comfort she needs to accept reality even when it is ugly, and to grieve all that has been lost in her own life as well as in the world. Thank you for her!"

SEPTEMBER 2015 – TRIP NUMBER 2 – I AM NOT ALONE

We called 911 for Allie last night. She was triggered after an intense therapy session and I found her cutting herself. I spent much of the night looking after her at the hospital before they admitted her.

Many times, the thought has crossed my mind that she could very well take her own life. How would I feel if this happened? Would it be my fault? Would she finally be at rest?

Recognizing the fearful thought, I connect relationally and find my appreciation memory. Jesus is there in the field of yellow flowers where I go to rest, play and receive from God.

"How do *I* cope through all of this? I know it always gets worse before it gets better. I just want to be stable for her during her ups and downs. How do I do it, Papa?"

I feel led to go outside to the trampoline. I follow my intuition without question. I have learned that sometimes our bodies know what we need, even if we do not have words for it. I lie down on my back, look up at the clouds, and thaw to worship music. The sky is gorgeous, the weather perfect.

The songs *I am not Alone, Forever,* and *Oceans Deep* accompany me as I let grief and fear fill my body, soul and mind. I feel Him with me on the trampoline. I glance over my shoulder and put out my hand to take His. We make eye contact. I am truly NOT alone. The fear disappears completely as I look in His eyes.

In the absence of fear, pain floods. Gratitude and grief, hand in hand. I look away, up to the clouds. We watch them again as they play our memories, our moments. I rest. I pray for my precious daughter.

After an hour or so of this, I sense in my imagination Jesus leading me from the field of yellow flowers into the forest where the wolves are. Allie, my daughter, is out there in the woods. She is exposed. Jesus carries light with us; it emanates from His very body. He *is* the light. As long as I stay with Him, in His light, I am safe.

He stops, turns to me and surprisingly names me again, "You are Toni, My precious restorer. You will restore to Me those who are broken."

"Is this even true?" I ask myself, wondering if I am just making all of this up in my own head.

"Believe what you see," I hear.

I see myself putting people's hands into the hands of Jesus. I see myself helping equip pastors, therapists, and counselors to better deal with trauma and mental illness.

Then, I see my Allie and wonder if she will ever be restored. Will her hands ever reach for His?

"What do you see?" He asks.

I look into the future, and again, I see her on the river bank with Jesus, laughing, enjoying, being enjoyed.

"Believe what you see," I hear again.

"But I am scared I will mess it up, say the wrong thing, or not share more of the right thing at the right time."

"Do you think I am limited by how you respond to her?" He lovingly laughs at the absurdity of that thought.

I join His laughter, recognizing how preposterous the idea sounds.

"I am so much bigger than all of that," He continues. "Trust Me. Follow Me. Listen to Me. Rest in Me."

Trust Me. These are some of the very first words I ever sensed my Lord saying to me. I am stayed. I am calmed. I am with Him, and He is everything. I am Toni Maria, precious sea of sorrow and strength. I am a restorer. And I must know my limits. He is The Restorer. I am simply the messenger delivering the message of reconciliation, putting one's hand into the hand of Jesus.

I come back to the present, to the clouds in the sky. I cannot help but smile. Jesus is with my Allie, and He is with me. The words "I am not alone" resound in my mind, in my body, and in my soul.

*****

During those most difficult years, more than ever, Allie needed me to parent fearlessly, believing that she would be okay no matter what. She needed a source of stability, faith and strength. The presence and perspective of God in the core of my being continually dismantled my fear so that I could ever so imperfectly co-create this stable foundation.

Allie knows she is deeply loved by God. At the writing of this book, she is almost 21 years old, fully independent and loving figuring out life through trial and error. Several times she has even been tempted to let God's love in. On occasion, she invites me to practice appreciation with her and invite Truth to come. She knows the pathway when she wants to take it. That is my job—to model for her, and all of my children, how to let God parent them, how to walk the path of the four Rs. It is their job to take the journey themselves and see that there is nothing, no nothing, beyond God's repair. There is nothing we cannot get through because we are glad to be together no matter what, and we have a Divine source that can restore all that is lost.

And still, on any given day that fear comes, I get to again recognize it is active, realize I am not alone, receive Truth, and respond by co-creating new realities. Only then, joy fueled and Jesus led, can I lead my children, recapture their attention and reaffirm their resilience.

"Mommy," 10-year-old Matt announced to the family just the other day, "I love where our family is right now."

"What do you mean, Sweetie," I asked, with a quick smile and glance at my husband.

"Well, I just love where we are emotionally and financially. We don't have too much or too little, but just enough to get by. And emotionally, we are all glad to be together and we just know we can get through anything. And that makes me happy!"

Resources

Parenting Fearlessly is not impossible, but it does require relationship, training, and community. Don't hesitate to reach out to www.LK10.com where a community of practice awaits you.

Back to Joy: An Intimate Journey with Jesus into Emotional Health and Maturity by Toni M. Daniels

This intensely personal book offers a different model for dealing with emotional struggles. Intimate journal entries spanning 18 years of Toni's missionary life will show you how Jesus gently led her back to joy and into health and maturity.

Joy Fueled: Catalyzing a Revolution of Joyful Communities by John C White, Toni M. Daniels, Dr. Kent Smith

This revolutionary, yet practical book seeks to ignite a movement of vibrant communities of Jesus by delivering three simple practices that inspire hope, build resilience, foster mature relationships and catalyze a self-propagating revolution of joy.

Joyful Journey: Listening to Immanuel by Wilder, Loppnow, Loppnow, Kang

Discover how you can enjoy daily guidance and friendship with God, using methods grounded in scripture, spiritual disciplines and cutting-edge neuroscience.

Appreciation Story Log: https://bit.ly/LK10 *appreciation*

Appreciation Story Log
(plus "act like myself" and Interactive story)
click here for Matt Daniels demonstrating

Day, Date: _____   Title (see #7): _____

Simple 2-min Appreciation Story

1. Briefly describe the situation:

2. How did I feel in this story. List feeling words:

3. How did I feel physically, in my body, during this story. List sensations and body location:

Act like myself Story

4. What actions did I do; responses did I have; or other reactions in this story that demonstrate "what it is like me" to do?: (If I did not "act like myself" at the time, how would have liked to have done this)

Interactive Appreciation Story

5. Thank God for that memory. Ask "Where are you in this memory God?" then, How did You feel about me / this?

6. Anything You want me to know about this memory? About me? About you? (then, "Anything else?")

7. Pick a word or a few words to "title" the memory. This will help draw back the totality of the experience:

Bonus: Tell one of these stories to someone today. Keep it to less than 3 minutes. As you tell the story, make eye contact, include feeling words, body sensation words, and how you like to act in this story. Not only will you make someone's day, you will also strengthen your bond with them and capacity for emotional resilience in the face of stress and challenges.

REAFFIRMING RESILIENCE THROUGH REFLECTION

- Review the Story of what happened.
- What was your favorite part?
- What part seemed most important?
- What did you do to help you get back to joy?
- How did you find Jesus?
- What questions did you ask Him?
- What is it like us to do when we feel overwhelmed?
- What will you do next time you feel overwhelmed? Or What will you do differently next time?
- Do you feel like you know how to find Jesus by yourself if you need to?

About the Author

TONI M. DANIELS has worked in Pastoral Counseling, Church Planting and Leadership Development for over 25 years offering international training workshops and relational, skill-based coaching.

After an 18-year missionary career as in Uruguay, SA, Toni has broadened her impact as Training Champion and Operations Director for LK10, a global Christian equipping organization. She is passionate about training, what she calls, "Emotional, Spiritual Ninja Warriors" spurring her to create the Podcast "Joy Fueled and Jesus Led" and co-author several books including *Joy Fueled: Catalyzing a Revolution of Joyful Communities.*

Toni has a BA in Sociology, an MA in Leadership Development and Church Planting, a diploma in Spiritual Direction, and a total of five years of skills-based relationship enhancement training from the International Trainer's Association, PREP,inc., and THRIVEtoday.

Toni loves being outdoors and building joy with family and friends, especially her husband, their four children, her poodle, Champagne, and kitten, Snow Paws.

Joy Fueled & Jesus Led

Where real life intersects with divine presence

YouTube: http://bit.ly/ToniYouTube

Podcast: https://anchor.fm/toni-m-daniels

URGENT PLEA!

Thank You for Purchasing
4 Keys to Parent Fearlessly!

I really appreciate all of your feedback, and
love hearing what you have to say.
Your input helps to make the next book better.
Please leave a helpful review on Amazon letting me know
what you thought of the book.

Thanks so much!!
~ Toni M Daniels

Made in the USA
Las Vegas, NV
10 May 2021